SOCIETY IS | | DISRUPTER IS
COMPLIANT → CURIOUS
CONFORMIST → CREATIVE
SUBSERVIENT → STRONG
OBEDIENT → ASSERTIVE
IMITATOR → INITIATOR
STAYING QUIET → SPEAKING UP
RIGID → EXPERIMENTAL
SUBMISSION TO STATUS QUO → INNOVATIVE STATUS GROW

Praise for
DISRUPT-HER

"In *Disrupt-Her*, Miki Agrawal invites all us humans to reexamine the beliefs and behaviors that keep us from living a fully expressed and authentic life. If you have ever wondered how to break free of group think and be who you are, read this book. In a world where more of us need to live in a way that adds to goodness, creativity, and innovation, this book is your guide."

— MARK HYMAN, M.D., #1 *New York Times* best-selling author of *Food: What the Heck Should I Eat?* and director, Cleveland Clinic Center for Functional Medicine

"Any time a woman says to a system that doesn't work for her, for her children, for any species or for the planet, *No, no way, not gonna, I've had it—that way of doing things doesn't work for me so don't even think about asking me*, I say, 'You go girl!' So to Miki Agrawal: 'You go girl, and please keep going!'"

— MARIANNE WILLIAMSON, #1 *New York Times* best-selling author of *A Return to Love*

"An important book written at an important time, *Disrupt-Her* forces us to question all that is not serving us in our own life and in the greater society. A must-read!"

— JOHN MACKEY, co-founder and CEO of Whole Foods Market and author of *Conscious Capitalism* and *The Whole Foods Diet*

"I needed to read this. I needed these exact words after a year of feeling like a victim and a blamer who can't change her life or circumstances. This miracle of writing . . . is a fucking game changer."

— STACY LONDON, editor, activist, stylist, and former co-host of *What Not to Wear*

"This book is actually a manifesto meant for anyone who is bumping up against the edges of the typical societal mold and wondering if there's more to life. Miki shows us that if we run toward our authentic selves, indeed, there is."

— SOPHIA BUSH, actress and activist

"If you want to flip the bird at the Patriarchy and outdated preconceptions, and then shift into your own power, read this book."

— RICKI LAKE, filmmaker and co-creator of *The Business of Being Born* and *Weed the People*

"This book shifts our perspective and acts as a forcing function to question what changes we need to make in each of our lives, and how to best act with a sense of urgency."

— HARLEY FINKELSTEIN, COO of Shopify and Dragon from Dragons' Den

"Miki's book *Disrupt-Her* is a one-of-a-kind manifesto that takes you by the hand, energetically pulls you away from societal preconceptions, and pushes you toward a life and world of possibility and abundance where you will shout, 'YES!! I CAN DO ANYTHING!' Miki lived through all the ups and downs of being a Disrupt-her and emerges with this book and perspective of life that is vulnerable, POWERFUL, and contagious. She was born to write this book. Get it and it will change your life."

— RADHA AGRAWAL, founder and CEO of Daybreaker.com and author of *Belong*

"*Disrupt-Her* is a book that will upgrade your mental conditioning and help you rethink your life from top to bottom."

— JIM KWIK, celebrity brain coach and founder, Kwik Learning

"*Disrupt-Her* helps you rethink your belief systems, challenge your societal conditioning, and provide tools to live exactly the way you want. It will allow you to create new, up-leveling possibilities for yourself in a fun, engaging, story-driven *and* research-driven way. Read this book and watch your life shift for the better."

— JACK CANFIELD, co-author of *Chicken Soup for the Soul* and *The Success Principles*

"Miki goes straight to the truth and there is no wiggle room for any kind of excuses. Her powerful lessons are based on her personal journey as well as fact-based research, which will inspire you to want to put the book down and start acting immediately. It's a powerful, truthful fire lit directly under your ass."

— SUZY BATIZ, founder and CEO, Poo-Pourri and Supernatural

"If you want to shift away from societal conditioning and shift into your authentic power, read this book. As a female CEO and founder, I found this book truly inspiring and it moved me into high gear with my own creativity and projects."

— LAYLA MARTIN, #1 conscious sexuality expert

"As a societal-norm-buster too, I really relate to this book because it forces everyone to rethink all of their old belief patterns and gives them the room to create their own fresh perspective. Highly recommend!"

— ASA AKIRA, award-winning porn star, author of *Insatiable*, and popular podcaster

"In an era where leadership inspired from the femme archetype is needed more than ever, *Disrupt-Her* comes at the perfect time, inspiring us to question problematic societal norms, deconstruct archaic social stigmas, and prioritize how to come as our most authentic selves."

— MADAME GANDHI, musician/activist

"*Disrupt-Her* is a perfectly timed and wildly bold call to arms. To all fellow builders and earth shakers: please run, grab your gumption, and consume this book!"

— LAUREN HANDEL ZANDER, author of *Maybe It's You* and co-founder and chairwoman, Handel Group

DISRUPT-HER

ALSO BY MIKI AGRAWAL

Do Cool Sh*t

DISRUPT-HER

A MANIFESTO FOR THE MODERN WOMAN

MIKI AGRAWAL

HAY HOUSE, INC.

Carlsbad, California • New York City
London • Sydney • New Delhi

Published in the United States by: Hay House, Inc.: www.hayhouse.com®
Published in Australia by: Hay House Australia Pty. Ltd.: www.hayhouse.com.au
Published in the United Kingdom by: Hay House UK, Ltd.: www.hayhouse.co.uk
Published in India by: Hay House Publishers India: www.hayhouse.co.in

Cover design: Taylor Franklin
Interior design: Charles McStravick
Interior illustrations: Courtesy of the author
Photo spreads with artwork: Photography by Daniel Johnson; artwork by Taylor Franklin
Photo on page vii: Andrew Horn
Photo on page 242: Bridget Collins
Photo on page 274: Daniel Johnson

LIBRARY OF CONGRESS CATALOGING-IN-PUBLICATION DATA

Names: Agrawal, Miki, author.
Title: Disrupt-her : a manifesto for the modern woman / Miki Agrawal.
Other titles: Disrupt her
Description: 1st edition. | Carlsbad, California : Hay House, [2018] |
   Includes bibliographical references.
Identifiers: LCCN 2018034069 | ISBN 9781401955564 (hardcover : alk. paper)
Subjects: LCSH: Self-realization in women. | Change (Psychology) | Attitude
   change. | Women--Psychology.
Classification: LCC HQ1206 .A27 2018 | DDC 646.70082--dc23 LC record available at
https://lccn.loc.gov/2018034069

Hardcover ISBN: 978-1-4019-5556-4
E-book ISBN: 978-1-4019-5557-1
Audiobook ISBN: 978-1-4019-5594-6
10 9 8 7 6 5 4 3 2 1
1st edition, January 2019

33614080861692

PRINTED IN THE UNITED STATES OF AMERICA

This book is dedicated to
my new, incredible, dimply-bootied,
adventurous, curious, smiley, sometimes loud,
sometimes soft, fully engaged son Hiro Happy.

Hiro, I promise to never lose myself for you,
because the more ME I can be,
the more I can inspire you to be YOU.
You GOT this!

A NOTE TO YOU

By opening this book, you are opening yourself up to disrupting much of what you believe to be "true" in the world so you can live your most vibrant, strong, actualized, lit-up life **ever**. Congratulations for taking this big, courageous step.

Disrupt-Her has "Her" in it, implying it's written for women only, but "he" is within "her," much like "man" is within "woman."

The Bible speaks of "man," Aristotle writes about "man," and even Viktor Frankl wrote *Man's Search for Meaning*, yet women read those texts too, don't they? So why can't we say "her" and "woman" and have men read it too? We can.

This book *was* written by a woman, for women, but it's meant to be read by all humans. So when I refer to "her," it does include YOU too, if you so choose.

dictionary
inflection

wom·an
wo·man

inclusive
inflection

NO MATTER WHO YOU ARE, PLEASE READ FROM AN OPEN, SELF-INQUIRING PERSPECTIVE.

CONTENTS

INTRODUCTION

"Miki and Radha, the principal would like to see you in his office, please."

As my twin sister and I sat in the principal's office, our feet dangling off our chairs, the enormous principal, with his booming voice, entered the room and said:

"It has been brought to my attention that you two are being disruptive in class and at recess. The teacher said that you've been talking in class and playing King of the Mountain with the boys."

This was wintertime in Montreal, and the shoveled snow created massive mounds that allowed the kids to play King of the

Mountain and attempt to push each other off the piles of snow. It was always only boys playing the game, and our 10-year-old selves had decided that *we* wanted to conquer the mountain that day.

Radha and I looked at each other proudly. We (a) loved talking and (b) had so much fun playfully pushing the boys off the mountain.

We gleefully responded, "Oh yes! We became the queens of the mountain today! Do we get a trophy for being the *first* queens of the mountain?!"

The principal responded sternly, "That's not funny. You can't do that anymore. You can't push the boys off the mountain. It will give them a complex."

"A complex? What's a complex?" This was the first time I had ever heard the word.

"They will become insecure because the girls are pushing them around." Really. He said that.

"Wait, what's wrong with that?" I asked.

"Stop being funny," he said, his eyes boring into me. "NEVER. DO. IT. AGAIN."

Twenty-eight years later.
New York City.
The office of *Forbes* magazine.

"Really, Miki? A company called TUSHY? That makes bidets? Of all the companies to start next, why would you start this?" The reporter looked at me, puzzled.

TUSHY

I laughed, mostly at myself. If only she knew all the bloody details of what it took to build my previous company, THINX. From the four years of not getting paid to create a best-in-class period-proof underwear product with my co-founders, to the inability to raise money at first because pretty much all investors were men (who definitely did *not* want to be talking about periods), to the struggle of getting the business off the ground when skeptical women talked shit about the product before even trying it ("What do you mean, *bleed* in my underwear? Ha! I'll never use this product!"), to going viral internationally after defeating the New York City public transit system's attempts to ban our period advertisements in the subways, to incredulously growing the company exponentially with my team over a two-and-a-half-year period to a valuation of over $100 million, to making typical start-up-founder-scaling-very-fast mistakes (which includes being hotheaded), to then getting taken down ruthlessly by the media for an inflamed allegation that was subsequently withdrawn, to a final decision for me to step down as C.E.O. while I was six months pregnant . . .

. . . So to *really* answer the reporter's question, it actually *did* seem a little insane to try to disrupt yet another taboo category with a product that society wasn't quite ready to talk about, *again*: TUSHY (hellotushy.com, not to be confused with the porn site—lol).

I replied: "Because nobody is innovating in the toilet space, wiping your butt with dry paper is gross, toilet paper is *still* killing 15 million trees per year, causing major environmental issues, and the global sanitation crisis is one of humanity's greatest killers on the planet . . . and I think my team and I can do something about it."

And then I added: "I also now know to expect *all* that comes with being a Disrupt-Her, both good and bad, and I want to see how I fare the next go-round. Plus, I want to show myself, and other women too, that we can *always* stand back up proudly, even after we screw up or get pushed around and beaten up badly. It's probably the most important part of being a Disrupt-Her."

SO WHAT IS A DISRUPT-HER?

The word "disrupter" has had a negative connotation in society ever since the English language gave it a definition. Synonyms you will find are "anarchist," "troublemaker," "malcontent," "rebel," "instigator"—these have all been mostly used to define the "bad guys" in media or in culture.

In fact, the literal definition of "disrupt" is "to destroy temporarily" or "to break apart" or "to throw in turmoil or disorder" or "to interrupt."

But what if you read the word "disrupter" and its synonyms with a smile on your face? (Try it!) What if you read them from the perspective of important, positive, forward-thinking change? What if it was purposeful disruption? Without the breaking-apart / interrupting / throwing-into-turmoil mentality, progress will never happen.

Society, by contrast, will always push back against disruptive change, purposeful or not. And it gives darn good reasons for you to stay where you are and uses tactics to make you wonder why you even questioned it in the first place.

After all, their method is "proven" to give us a semblance of security and order, which are both qualities that humans do long for. Society has tricked us into believing that what it is saying is truth or reality or "just how things are" because it's been "proven" by past generations.

We often don't think any of it can be changed or evolve, but **it all can.**

The same status-quo thinking goes for companies too. You get your paycheck every two weeks, so you believe inherently that all the usual practices and procedures are "just the way things are done here." The company has been around for years, so it must have all of its ducks in a row, right?

The same goes for your daily existence. Things like wiping your butt with dry toilet paper after you poop or using societally accepted consumable products that have been around for years are, again, "just the way you do things," and you don't question it.

If you do have the impulse to go against society, you may also remember that society will sometimes use drastic measures to maintain its form. Socrates and Galileo were ridiculed and called fools, Jesus Christ was crucified, and Joan of Arc was burned alive. Makes you second-guess yourself, right?

Now, why should you even care about questioning things, because you think you're "pretty happy" where you are? You'd rather NOT be burned alive, thank you very much. I get that.

Well, the truth is that today, according to Gallup, 70 percent of American adults hate their jobs,[1] more people are on antidepressants and are lonelier than ever before, and more and more humans are making unconscious decisions that are hurting our only home: Planet Earth . . . even though we all say we strive to be happy and *want* to raise our children to be happy on a happy Earth.

So *clearly*, we *don't* believe what is societally accepted as "truth." We don't *really* want a safe life filled with more stuff that bogs us down, we don't *really* want to follow a "career path" that is "sensible," and we certainly don't want to meet up with "Sally" every Sunday at the same brunch spot and bitch about our relationships, work, and the latest antics of [insert name of celebrity or public figure]. We don't *really* want any of those things, do we?

What we *actually* want is to do what we *want* to do (or at least to spend our precious time figuring out what that is), and do it fully lit up and wholeheartedly ourselves! We know that life is so fleeting, and we want to break out of following a ready-made path like obedient sheep. But we often don't quite know where to begin.

Well, that's what this book will help you do! Figure out how to break out of the mold, question where you are being inauthentic and why, and then DISRUPT the SH** out of all those places, in the most exciting way imaginable.

START RIGHT NOW!

Being disruptive begins the moment we realize that "society" was created by *people* who are no different than any of us, and in that instant, we understand that we can *choose* to change everything, to morph all our "society-said-you-shoulds" into exactly what we want, creating entirely new possibilities for ourselves that will provide complete, embodied fulfillment for the rest of our lives.

I can't think of a better time than RIGHT NOW to get started—can you? Every moment we spend living an inauthentic life and following made-up rules is a moment we could have experienced in our full, authentic power.

So let's question, challenge, and take action, shall we?

Oh, and before you write off this idea, thinking you can't be a disrupter because you have X, Y, and Z responsibilities and "it's only for people who have money or time or *no* adult responsibilities," or because you too have been conned by society into believing that their method is truth, or because you're "too busy to make any changes," or because you have another story you choose to believe, I'm here to tell you that it doesn't have to be "either / or"; it can be "yes and." You CAN have security and order and STILL be a disrupter.

The Socrateses, Jesus Christs, Joan of Arcs, and Galileos of the world are the people we remember to this day and will remember throughout history because they inspired us to live our own truth, not anyone else's, and to question everything. They are the ones who forged ahead and came up with new ideas and ways of thinking despite the pressures of herd mentality.

WHY "HER" IN "DISRUPT-HER"?

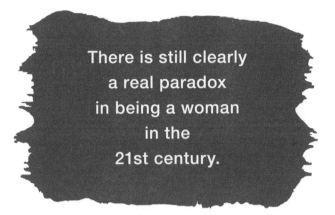

There is still clearly
a real paradox
in being a woman
in the
21st century.

We have our periods and are looked down on for being emotional during our cycles ("She's so PMS-y right now"); and yet when we are emotionless, we are considered "manly" and "icy."

We are told to be stick skinny, and yet we are judged for not having voluptuous breasts or big butts.

If we don't speak up, it's "our fault" that we didn't get the promotion, the position, the project, or the pay raise, and if we do speak up and go for it, we're "pushy" or "bitchy."

We are judged for being working women and not being there for our children, and yet we are also judged for being stay-at-home moms and not working. We are also judged if we aren't mothers at all.

Perhaps the greatest paradox of all is that **women give birth to all men (and all humans) and**, after being held inside our wombs for nine months, birthed, breastfed, and often raised primarily by women, **some men turn around and oppress women, especially in certain parts of the world.** This is one of the biggest disconnections of our time that needs a massive transformational shift.

Women in America only got the right to vote in 1920, and in most of the world women are considered inferior to men. Ninety-five percent of C.E.O.s of for-profit organizations are men. There has never been a female American president. And yet *all* men *come* from women!

And now, according to a new report from the Center for American Progress, "42% of mothers were the sole or primary family breadwinner last year. An additional 22% were co-breadwinners."[2] So 64 percent of women now are either primary or co-breadwinners, on top of giving birth to all men, and we're *still* living in a patriarchal society?

> *Change the status quo*
> *or become it.*
> MARK SHAYLER

I too have experienced the good, the awesome, and the ugly while launching and growing my companies, pushing the boundaries of female leadership and what's acceptable in society. I've created innovations in the categories of periods, pee, and poop, and talking about these things has made many people very uncomfortable. I've had to overcome societal stigmas, cultural taboos, grossed-out male investors, and the double standards of female leadership. My goal here is to share all the lessons I've learned along the way.

I have also faced major patriarchal pushback and experienced firsthand attempts to keep a female leader "in check" and not "too disruptive" or "too strong." I had a choice to either quiet myself and shrink to what's acceptable to society or continue to push boundaries and speak up productively—and I chose the latter, because it's all part of the challenge of being a Disrupt-Her. I deeply believe that everything happens *for us*, not *to us*, and if we can take all parts of our journey—the good and the bad—with the same hunger for knowledge and willingness to dissect what worked and what didn't, then all of it will be a blessing in the end.

"DISRUPT-HER" DEFINED

A Disrupt-Her questions everything in her own life, in culture, and in society to ensure that she is maximizing her life experiences before it's all over like a flash in the pan.

A Disrupt-Her understands that there are only about 21,000 days to live from the point when we graduate college (usually at around 22 years old) to the point when we die (around the average age of 80), and she deeply gets that time is the most nonrenewable resource we have. Thus, she is laser focused on creating the most value for herself, her community, and the world while she is here for said short amount of time. Like Thoreau, she wants to "live deep and suck out all the marrow of life."[3]

So with our mortality in mind (or as I like to call it, "the holy shitness of being alive"), a Disrupt-Her is unafraid to charge forward and try new things, even if the terrain ahead is rocky and uncertain. She is bold and proud to be fully embodied as herself, flaws and all; she speaks up and shares her thoughts, even if society might be trying to squelch her "new kind of thinking." A Disrupt-Her doesn't have "fail" or "failure" in her vocabulary; she sees every experience only as an opportunity to learn and grow—and she prides herself on making any attempt at all in her passionate pursuits. A Disrupt-Her knows that Hate-Hers exist who want to take her down but also that Love-Hers exist who want to champion her in her pursuits. A Disrupt-Her also knows that Hate-Hers are only Hate-Hers when they're hurt themselves, so she's learned not to take it too personally. A Disrupt-Her who has children believes that being a mother should be on her résumé (rather than being seen as a detriment at the office), knowing that she can take care of another life selflessly, around the clock, even if she's sick or exhausted; can multitask; and is very efficient with her time.

Only when we question, challenge, and then disrupt all aspects of our lives can we live a more excited, impassioned, lit-up existence filled with adventure, love, friendship, and fulfilling work that creates a positive ripple effect for generations to come.

You are about to walk away
with 13 major disruptions in
your personal and professional life
that can light you up, put a lasting pep
and purpose in your step, and have
genuine, transformative, positive
effects on everything you do.
Each chapter will begin with a common belief
that is currently "accepted by society,"
and these will be disrupted one by one.
There will also be questions at the end
of every chapter that will give you
the opportunity to apply what you've just
read to your own circumstances,
so you can produce real-world results.

Before turning the
page,
PRESS HERE

to eliminate all self-
judgment + judgment
of others.

DISRUPT-HER

SURPRISE!

BEFORE WE GET TO THE
13 DISRUPTIONS IN YOUR LIFE ...

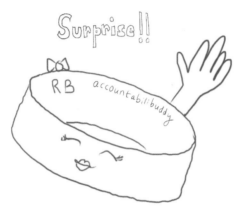

Meet RB the rubber band! She is ready to wake up now. (You can either buy a white rubber band anywhere online or you can get one at Disrupther.co.) She asks that you put her on your **RIGHT WRIST** to give you extra confidence that you made the **RIGHT DECISION** in wanting to disrupt your life in the most positive, daring way possible.

Going cold turkey on judging ourselves and others is **HARD**, and your current self will fight hard to avoid change and might think with an eye roll, *I'm too old for this rubber band kid shit*, but RB will be your loving **ACCOUNTABILIBUDDY** and will help you laugh through this journey. Her full name is **ARE-BE (RB for short!)** and she is here to help you assess who you **ARE** today, figure out what you believe in, both personally and professionally, question why you believe those things, and stay accountable to who you want to **BE** moving forward in all aspects of your life.

She will be the one asking you to do things at the end of each chapter, so say hello to your new imaginary best friend! Have fun!

DISRUPTION #1

We have to "get serious"
as we grow up.

You can still live in a childlike state
of curiosity, playfulness, and awe
and be a responsible adult
at the same time.

Every child is an artist.
The problem is how to remain an artist
once [s]he grows up.

attributed to
PABLO PICASSO

"On your maaaaaark!" (said with a thick Indian accent)

Long pause for dramatic effect.

"Geeeeet seeeeeettttt!" (with an even thicker Indian accent)

An even longer pause.

My father gleefully held a whistle in his fingers, waiting. As soon as we contestants all turned to look at him, wondering why it was taking him so long to blow the damn whistle—BEEEEP!—he blew the whistle as loud as he could.

It was 2005 and we were at our 10th annual family barbecue (affectionately called Agra-Palooza). My twin sister, Radha, and I were defending our three-legged race championship title (unde-feated for, *ahem*, nine consecutive years, might I add). Granted, we had a serious advantage over all the other teams, including our older sister, Yuri, because identical twins in this game are basically clones tethered together.

"One, two! One, two!"
"Start with your left foot forward at the turn!!"
"Let's go!!!"
Four turns back and forth on our lawn, and we were going to defeat the five other finalists and clinch our 10th annual title for some MAJOR bragging rights.

As we one-two-ed down the lawn in the lead, all of a sudden, halfway through the race, the unexpected happened.
BLOOD.
EVERYWHERE . . .

Okay, fine, blood wasn't everywhere. And it wasn't a dramatic accident with broken body parts.

"Ack! I just started my period!" Radha yelled.
"Noooooo!" I yelled back.
Radha immediately started bleeding through her bathing suit and down her legs onto her socks . . . onto MY sock too, because we were tied together.

We made the obvious decision: to just keep going. We sprinted through the finish line (in first place . . . had to say it) and then, still tied to each other, we kept running as fast as we could, but this time it was up the stairs to our bathroom so Radha could change out of her bathing suit.

"Ugh, on my favorite bathing suit!"

As I watched her wash the blood out in the sink, the ding ding ding sound of a BIG IDEA started ringing in my head.

"What if we could create a pair of beautiful, simple underwear that never stained and never leaked?" I said to Radha. "Wouldn't it be amazing if there was underwear you could just wash out instead of them being stained forever or so ruined you have to throw them away? Even better, what if the underwear absorbed the blood?" Right at that moment, our entrepreneurial mind kicked into full gear. We started brainstorming tag lines like "No stains. No leaks. Period." We immediately wrote the idea down.

Nobody in that moment would have guessed that this idea, born out of a three-legged race at Agra-Palooza, would grow into a multimillion-dollar enterprise a few years later and transform the lives of millions of women globally. Our THINX concept might never have been birthed had we not created a container of playfulness for ourselves as adults.

People often say that our children are our greatest teachers because of the purity of their minds. The same goes in the business world—fresh new ideas often come when we are stripped down to simply playing "like children."

WHEN DID WE ACTUALLY GO FROM "#AWE-ING" LIKE CHILDREN TO "#ADULTING"?

"#AWE-ING" DEFINED:
A state of childlike curiosity,
playfulness, and awe. Creativity is copious.
Joyful exclamations like "Oooh!" are aplenty.
Playing is constructive and adds to the world.
There is no self-consciousness here,
so flow state is abundant.

"#ADULTING" DEFINED:
Being a responsible adult who
pays the bills and abides by societally
accepted practices like getting a 30-year fixed
mortgage or not talking to anyone on the subway.
Society has placed judgments on how people
should look and act, so people are much more
self-conscious in the #adulting state, which
often prevents true, authentic flow.

"Okay, you grab Ganzy and I'll grab Skippy." Skippy the chipmunk was my favorite stuffed animal and Ganzy the bear was Radha's favorite stuffed animal. "Skippy and Ganzy are in outer space and they are flying through the sky and see an alien friend and they start talking and become best friends, and the alien—let's call her Ali—invites Skippy and Ganzy to her house and shows us all the slimy stuff she eats." I barely took a sip of air in between words as I came up with the whole storyline and talked as fast as I could.

Radha followed up excitedly: "Yes, exactly—and then Ali takes us to meet her family and they all sing us a song." The song went something like this: "Fejfepwomi'repibnevoimvolmrw." She sang at the top of her lungs.

And the story went on and on, and our five-year-old selves played for hours with just our little stuffed toys in our hands, giggling and having the best time.

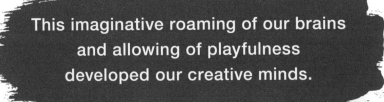

This imaginative roaming of our brains and allowing of playfulness developed our creative minds.

Remember when we were kids and all we wanted to do was sing, play hide-and-seek, stick our feet in the mud, play sports, do arts and crafts, and HAVE FUN? Remember when we didn't care about what was "cool" or "socially acceptable," because we didn't even know what that meant? We cried when we were hungry or hurt, and we got over it in a flash. We laughed LOUDLY at everything we thought was funny, and we were endlessly curious about the world around us (like, how does the hair grow so long in Daddy's nose?). At this stage in our lives, we thought we could DO ANYTHING, BE ANYTHING. And we had no clue at all that there was any inequality between genders.

Until . . . a few years later, when we started hearing:
"You're not a little girl anymore. Stop playing around."
"Grow up."
"Get serious."
"Stop staring."
"Stop talking so loudly, please. Sit down and be quiet."
"Shhhhhhh."
All the innocent things we did as kids became "indecent" or "disruptive" as we got older.

"#AWE-ING" TO "#ADULTING"
FALL FROM GRACE CHART

Innocent ⟶ Indecent

Playful ⟶ Disruptive

Fun ⟶ Bad

And thus the "conditioning" began. And in more ways than one . . .

"Hi, Mrs. S!"

Radha and I loved visiting our girlfriend V's house so we could eat her mom's classic Greek food and play Super Mario Brothers (which we weren't allowed to play in our strict Asian household).

As we were finishing dinner, Mrs. S said: "Girls, I think it's time that I take you to my aesthetician to get your upper lips and eyebrows waxed. You're 15 years old now, and I think it's time you each start looking more like a lady. V has been doing it for over a year now, and she looks great!"

She said this with utmost love and care and truly wanted what was "best" for us. Radha and I definitely had some hair on our upper lips at the time since we were going through our hormonal adolescent phase and things were sprouting everywhere (#unibrow #slightmustache). It wasn't clear who was hairier, half Indians like us or Greeks. Our Japanese half certainly balanced things out a bit.

We hadn't realized that there was anything "wrong" with having a little hair until this moment. Mrs. S was the most loving, wonderful human, but she too was conditioning us to look a certain way because it was what conformed to society's adult female standards and what she was taught was most appealing to the opposite sex.

It was another "fall from grace" moment, when we went from not thinking about how we looked to suddenly being self-conscious about it. We realized then that society judged us and told us that if we had hair on our bodies, something was wrong.

So as we entered our teen years, we started to lose sight of our childlike curiosity, playfulness, and awe. The world around us began to put societal pressures on us. They started marketing things to us, like material possessions, products that impacted our body image, and boy craziness (yes, I did shave my legs for you, Ravi; thank you for never noticing). We started to get society's wagging finger telling us what we could and couldn't do and where boundaries were (don't talk about "periods" and "moist discharge"). We also started to see all these images of what women are "supposed to" look like from a sexual objectification standpoint.

Thus began destructive self-judgment and judgment of others.

And then, finally, adulthood, where the years of societal pile-on and brainwashing got put to work.

✳

My dad started laughing.

"You're like a Christmas cake!"

"Daddy, what does that mean?"

"Well, today is your 26th birthday."

"And what does that have to do with a Christmas cake?"

"Well, on the 26th of December, Christmas cakes are old and nobody wants them anymore." He started laughing harder. "We need to put your name in the Times of India in the marriage section with 'Green card guaranteed' to attract suitors!" He couldn't stop laughing.

"Hardy har."

It was meant to be a "harmless joke," but it made me feel self-conscious about my age and my lack of a "partner." It made me start thinking about it in the back of my head.

✳

At every age we were being conditioned by everyone around us and were led to believe that this was how it worked in the world and we had to abide by it. And by the time we got to adulthood, those thoughts became truths:

"You need to be married and have kids."

"You need a good-paying, stable job with benefits."

"Don't become an artist or a 'creative'—what does that even mean? It pays nothing and isn't a real job."

"You need to buy a house with a white picket fence."

"Settle down and have kids soon, or you'll be an old spinster with a cat. You don't want that."

In the #adulting phase of our lives, we start doing the things our parents did or taught us to think we should do: "This is how things are done as an adult," or "Do these three things and you'll have a nice, safe life." They're not wrong; these things worked for them, so they could speak confidently, and that self-assured tone gave us some semblance of security, right?

But things start to get really serious really quickly. The #awe-ing playfulness and fun that once was at the forefront of every-thing is now farther and farther in the rearview mirror.

Even Robert Provine, the "laughing scientist" (it's really a thing), found that babies laugh 300 times a day. Compare that to adults, who laugh an average of 20 times a day.[1]

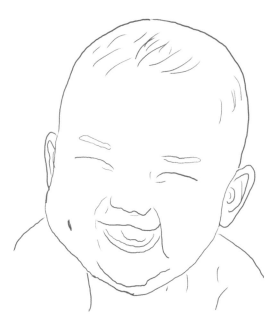

Unless we change course and create playful intentionality in the things we do, our adult lives can and will become mundane, predictable, and, well, unfunny.

So when you break it all the way down, going from #awe-ing (childlike playfulness, curiosity, and awe) to #adulting happened when we went from not caring about what other people and soci-ety thought about us (#awe-ing) to caring deeply about the way we're being judged and seen in the world (#adulting).

#Adulting doesn't happen overnight. It's a gradual death of confidence by a thousand paper cuts. These paper cuts could be anything from being told we can't do something or we shouldn't do something, to "don't push the boys off the mountain" because it's uncouth, taboo, not acceptable in society, or just plain "wrong." We get so much of other people's stuff piled onto us, like heavy cement, starting with our parents' issues, family judgments, neighborhood dramas, friends' theatrics, teachers' "sit down and shut up" broken records, school peer pressures, boss's set ways, media outrage, and society's "status quo." We start hearing, "Grow up," "Don't be silly," "You're making a fool of yourself," "Get your head out of the clouds," "Get serious," "Get real."

It's kind of hard to keep from dimming our childlike state of curiosity and awe when so much is piled on like this, right?

RUN "LIKE A GIRL": WHAT HAPPENS IF SOCIETAL THINKING TAKES OVER

"Show me what it looks like to run like a girl," the director of the commercial asked a 15-year-old girl.

The blond teenage girl in the commercial started running slowly, with her arms and legs flailing as though she were drowning and with her hair bouncing from side to side.

An older teenage brunette girl got asked the same question, and she also did a flail-y run and then grabbed her hair, dramatically saying, "My hair!" in a high-pitched tone.

An African American teenage girl got asked the same question and, giggling, ran with her arms fluttering like a goofy butterfly.

A 12-year-old boy and a 20-something man got asked the same question, and they too did the same "girly" motions described above.

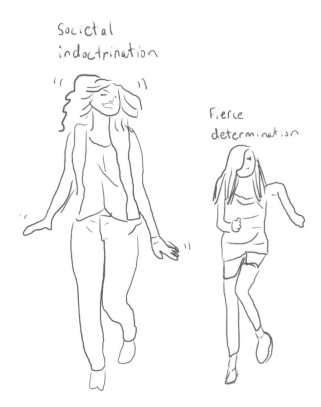

Societal indoctrination

Fierce determination

"Show me what it looks like to fight like a girl."

The 20-something man fluttered his arms weakly in front of him like he was swatting away bees in fast-forward. The teenage girls did a similar weak, fluttering hand motion.

"Now throw like a girl."

They each pretended to throw an imaginary ball all weird, flaily, and weak again.

The director of this commercial then brought in younger girls, under the age of 12, and asked them the exact same questions.

"Show me what it looks like to run like a girl."

The first 10-year-old, with determination on her face, ran as fast as she could. The same thing happened with an 11-year-old. She sprinted in place as fast as she could. A little 6-year-old dashed across the screen in a pink tutu as fast as she could too.

"Throw like a girl," the director instructed.

More preteen girls threw as hard as they could, with focused concentration on their faces.

"Fight like a girl."

These same young girls pretended to fight as hard as they could, with fierceness and determination.

"What do I mean when I say, 'Run like a girl'?" the director asked an 8-year-old girl.

"It means run as fast as you can," said the 8-year-old, matter-of-factly.

"Is 'like a girl' a good thing?" the director then asked a 12-year-old girl.

The 12-year-old was quiet at first and then said, "I actually don't know if it's a bad thing or a good thing. Sounds like a bad thing. Sounds like you're trying to humiliate someone."

The point of this commercial was to show that a girl's confidence plummets during puberty.

"So when they're in that vulnerable time, between the ages of 10 and 12, how do you think it affects them when somebody uses 'like a girl' as an insult?" the director asked the blond teenager.

The teen responded thoughtfully: "I think it definitely drops their self-confidence and really puts them down, because during that time, they're already trying to figure themselves out."

Then, once the director explained this to the first set of teenage girls, she asked them again to run, throw, and fight "like a girl." And they all did it again, but this time with their own fierceness, determination, and focus, as they would have done had they not learned the societal take on what "like a girl" meant. They went back to being who they were and believed in themselves again, just by being given permission to do so.

It was one of the most brilliant commercials, clearly showing how society truly impacts people from early on, especially girls and women, and if we don't change that train of thought as fast as possible, undoing the damage will require so much more effort. But if we notice why and how this is happening and catch this way of thinking before it permeates our thoughts, the undoing can happen.

#AWE-ING TO #ADULTING AND BACK TO THE #AWE-ING STATE

At my baby shower, when I received those hip, Brooklyn-chic children's books, wrapped in vintage burlap rope (and let's not forget the palo santo stick tucked inside the wrapping for added hipster effect), and was once again tickled by the fun, singsongy words with colorful, imaginative, hand-drawn pictures, I had another epiphany:

> If we're going to truly embody the Disrupt-Her, we need to first get ourselves back to the curious and playful *"#awe-ing state"* before the *"#adulting state"* took over.

So what happens in the #awe-ing state? Pre-existing judgments don't exist. In the #awe-ing state, we aren't self-conscious; we have endless fascination with everything around us, and we vocalize it. In the #awe-ing state, we run as fast as we can. In the #awe-ing state, we tell our daddy that he's balding and our mommy that she's gotten fat, without any filter, because it's just the plain truth. We say it without any preconceived societal negativity in our tone, which is why it doesn't hurt anyone's feelings. Nobody is ever outraged or shamed here, because how we say things is with pure matter-of-factness and loving wonder. In order for us to become true Disrupt-Hers in the #adulting state, we must be reborn without any preconceptions of how we (and others) "should" behave "as adults."

There really is a way to be responsible adults and also live in a state of genuine curiosity, playfulness, and awe.

WE ALL USED TO THINK WE WERE ARTISTS (ANOTHER EXAMPLE TO REALLY DRIVE THIS POINT HOME)

I know nothing with any certainty,
but the sight of the stars always
makes me dream.

VINCENT VAN GOGH

Gordon MacKenzie was one of the creative directors at Hallmark for 30 years. To keep himself in the #awe-ing state, he volunteered every month at an elementary school, to be among bright-eyed and bushy-tailed kids. He would ask the same question in each class: "How many artists are in the room?" Interestingly (though unsurprisingly), the responses changed as the grade levels went up.

The first graders would, MacKenzie wrote, "leap from their chairs, arms waving wildly, eager hands trying to reach the ceiling." All the children thought they were artists.

In the second-grade class, only half would raise their hands, "shoulder high, no higher, and the raised hands were still."

Among the third graders, only 10 kids out of 30 "tentatively, self-consciously" raised their hands.

The higher the grade, the smaller the number of children who raised their hands. By sixth grade, no more than one or two raised their hands and "did so ever so slightly—guardedly—their eyes glancing from side to side uneasily, betraying a fear of being identified by the group as a 'closet artist.'"[2]

Over the years when teachers and society told us to be quiet and get back in our seats, they thought they were doing their best to maintain order, but what they were also doing was stamping society's "be normal" and "don't be yourself" and "don't let your creative genius shine" brand onto us. Children get increasingly scared of authority and how society judges their creative genius. It becomes a vicious cycle to be more and more "normal."

Being a Disrupt-Her means you have to open back up the space in your brain that lets your childlike state of curiosity, playfulness, and awe come out, which will help allow your true genius and spirit to shine. Creating order is important to make a society run, but it shouldn't be achieved through self-consciousness tactics and by stifling people's true genius. There is space for it all.

THE IMPORTANCE OF FINDING PLACES TO PRACTICE #AWE-ING AS AN ADULT

"Come on, Andrew! Hurry!"

I biked across the playa at Burning Man 2017, excited to look at all the art people had put up all over the desert. This is one of my favorite rituals every year—to drink in the creativity of our fellow humans. None of the art had anyone's name on it or a logo of any kind, as one of the Burning Man commandments is "De-commodification." It isn't about egos or recognition; it is all about putting art in the world for the sake of putting art in the world and for radical self-expression. There was a massive doll that was five stories high and moved like a marionette; there were art cars in every shape, from a "disco space shuttle" to a massive unicorn;

there was a gorgeous, lifelike tree called Tree of Ténéré with green leaves during the day that lit up in every color of the rainbow at night. Art was sprawled all over the Burning Man grounds, ranging from big to small, elaborate to simple.

We bumped into a random art installation in the middle of the desert on our adventure: a lone washing machine with a fake cat sleeping on top of it. The cat had a mechanical system inside that made it look like it was breathing.

Cat sleeping on washing machine

I was so tickled by this funny installation that I sat on top of the washing machine to experience it on the playa.

All of a sudden, a stranger appeared on his bike with two friends and approached me.

"Are you having problems with your load too?" he asked.

He carried on without letting me answer.

"Because I kept trying, and the clothes were still wet, so I abandoned my load." He pulled out some chewing gum, unwrapped it, and put it inside the detergent drawer in the washing machine.

"Let me see if this works; because someone over there told me that this would do the trick. It apparently worked for him."

He was carrying on like we were having a real conversation, but he was making it all up as he went.

I giggled throughout the whole interaction and realized that in the "real world," this guy would have seemed completely crazy, but in this quirky place, his whimsy was welcomed and seen as a breath of fresh air.

> I was so delighted by this experience. And it was in this moment that I realized how important CONTEXT is in the world. We are "allowed" to be whimsical as kids, on theatrical stages, or at places like Burning Man, because society deems it "acceptable" in those contextual places. But as adults in the context of the "real world," we have to act a different way, based on society's rules. Context determines how and where to behave.

Imagine if we could be tickled by these kinds of theatrics in the real world without thinking the guy has lost his marbles. Imagine if we didn't judge others as harshly as we usually do, because we too get wrapped in the way things are "supposed to be" in this world. Imagine if we stopped judging others—then perhaps we'd stop judging ourselves and thus give ourselves permission to be exactly who we want to be and show up exactly how we want to show up in the world. We are all fluid beings, but society has made it so hard for us to show up exactly how we want to be in different contexts. These "societal guidelines" are all mirages; they don't exist, they're simply constructs that we CHOOSE to believe.

I go back to Burning Man every year because my creative inspiration tank gets filled up and my thinking about "social constructs" resets during this experience. Being playful and whimsical is integral to my creative process in all my businesses and in life, and I am most creative and most alive when there are no boundaries (or only loving ones) for me to play in as an adult.

PUTTING IT ALL TOGETHER

The intuitive mind is a sacred gift and the rational mind is a faithful servant. We have created a society that honors the servant and has forgotten the gift.

BOB SAMPLES,
The Metaphoric Mind

I wanted to drive this disruption home with quite a few examples, because this "#adulting thinking" is the most ingrained in us. It has to be untangled like a long necklace with so many knots in it that it's hard to know where to begin.

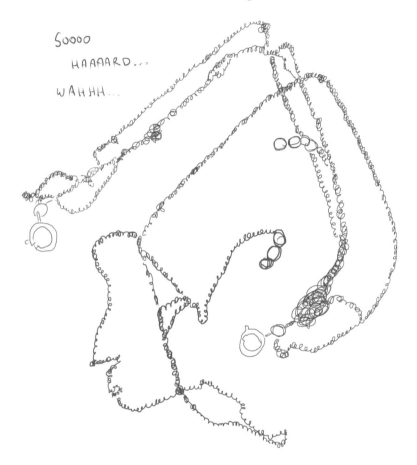

Soooo

HAAAARD...

WAHHH...

Let's recap.

As we become adults, society's conditioning takes us out of the #awe-ing state and puts us into the box of what is deemed to be "acceptable" according to its made-up standards. Historically society has valued productivity more than play because it's what brings us wealth and stability. As a founder and C.E.O. of several companies, both past and present, I get the importance of being productive and the need to get good work done to maintain a level of stability in business. But the Disrupt-Her in us also needs to break out of the conditional, judgmental #adulting state and into an #awe-ing state that supports being wholly ourselves—whimsical, creative, curious, playful, wonder-filled, and unique—which actually in turn helps us think more clearly about the work we are doing and about our lives overall. Aren't we generally able to think more clearly and creatively when we are most ourselves, not trying to be someone else or fit into a societally accepted box? A Disrupt-Her values BOTH tangible productivity and the more intangible elements of playfulness.

This is about disrupting our mind-set more than our actual work habits. It's not about having more vacation days, more free time, and getting away from work to "hang out" in a non-intentional way. There must be intentionality in our playing, even if the intention is to "do nothing" so our minds can gain space to think most clearly and creatively.

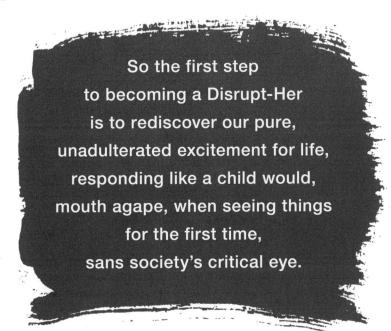

So the first step
to becoming a Disrupt-Her
is to rediscover our pure,
unadulterated excitement for life,
responding like a child would,
mouth agape, when seeing things
for the first time,
sans society's critical eye.

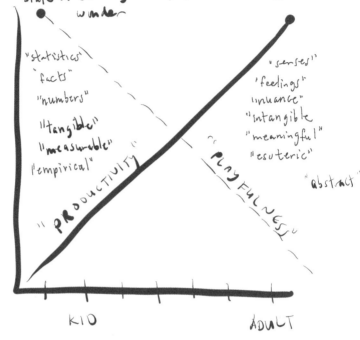

INTERNAL
INTUITIVE

EXTERNAL
SOCIETAL

childlike
state of curiosity +
wonder

responsible
adult

←→

WHAT
SOCIETY
VALUES

"statistics"
"facts"
"numbers"
"tangible"
"measurable"
"empirical"

"senses"
"feelings"
"nuance"
"intangible"
"meaningful"
"esoteric"
"abstract"

"PRODUCTIVITY"

"PLAYFULNESS"

KID

ADULT

AGE

We must value both.
To the degree we are disruptive
is when we honor both productivity +
playfulness.

DISRUPTION #1

EXERCISE

Please answer the following questions (on your own, with a Disrupt-Her partner, or in a group):

1. Can you share a story where your childlike state of curiosity, playfulness, and awe (your #awe-ing state) came out as a kid?

2. Can you share a story where your #awe-ing state came out as an adult?

3. Who taught you how to play? Or did you discover it somehow yourself?

4. Who in your life currently encourages you to live in an #awe-ing state and supports your dreaming?

5. Who in your work life brings out the #awe-ing state in you?

RB ACCOUNTABILIBUDDY
ACTION #1!

**THIS IS A TEST TO SEE HOW
PLAYFUL YOU CAN BE.**

TO KEEP YOU IN THE #AWE-ING STATE,
RB IS ASKING YOU TO TAKE THE FOLLOWING ACTION,
WHICH MAY FEEL FOREIGN (AND/OR WEIRD) TO YOU,
BUT IT WILL HELP ANCHOR THE LESSONS OF THIS CHAPTER
IN A PHYSICAL ACTION SO YOUR BODY
CAN INTERNALIZE WHAT YOUR MIND
IS LEARNING.

EVERY TIME YOU TAKE YOURSELF
SERIOUSLY OR FEEL YOURSELF
#ADULTING TOO HARD
AND NEED TO GET BACK TO YOUR
#AWE-ING STATE, PLEASE PUFF OUT
YOUR CHEEKS, LIKE THIS:

THEN PUT YOUR HANDS ON EITHER SIDE OF YOUR
FACE
AND POP YOUR PUFFED-OUT CHEEKS LOUDLY,
MAKING A FART-LIKE SOUND. THIS IS A
GREAT REMINDER THAT IT'S TIME
TO GET BACK TO YOUR CHILDLIKE STATE OF
CURIOSITY, PLAYFULNESS, AND AWE!
DON'T TAKE YOURSELF TOO SERIOUSLY!
SOCIETY ALREADY DOES THAT FOR YOU.

SEE HOW MANY TIMES YOU GET
TOO SERIOUS IN A DAY.

DISRUPTION #2

More stuff = a better life.

Clean house!
Practice addition by subtraction.

"That's all you need in life, a little place for your stuff."

This is my favorite George Carlin bit in his stand-up comedy repertoire.

"That's all your house is—a place to keep your stuff. If you didn't have so much stuff, you wouldn't need a house. You could just walk around all the time. A house is just a pile of stuff with a cover on it."

I can picture him in his brown sweater with his salt-and-pepper-bearded half grin on his face as he's talking. (It's worth You-Tubing it—search "George Carlin, stuff.")

"You can see that when you're taking off in an airplane. You look down, you see everybody's got a little pile of stuff. All the little piles of stuff.

"And when you leave your house, you gotta lock it up. Wouldn't want somebody to come by and take some of your stuff. They always take the *good* stuff. They never bother with that crap you're saving. All they want is the shiny stuff.

"That's what your house is, a place to keep your stuff while you go out and get . . . *more stuff*! "Sometimes you gotta move, gotta get a bigger house. Why? No room for your stuff anymore."

So true, right? And doesn't the word "stuff" feel so heavy after reading that?

WHEN DID SOCIETY BECOME SO OBSESSED WITH STUFF, ANYWAY?

Let's zoom out and go back in time for a sec.

During the Industrial Revolution (1760 to 1840-ish), when the assembly line and factories were forming (making stuff much cheaper to produce and to own), the people who ran these factories had to figure out how to get **more people** to (a) **make stuff** efficiently and obediently, and (b) **buy more stuff**. (That is, people had to learn how to go from owning only two pairs of shoes and one pair of pants to a closet full of stuff they don't need.) Since stuff was able to be mass-produced cost-effectively now, people had to *learn* to own more stuff.

Public schools (initially created by Horace Mann as "common schools" in the 1830s) were a big part of churning out good factory workers who could follow orders and be indoctrinated by a consumerist mind-set, so it's not an accident that this mandatory education happened during the time that factories were booming.

Mann's original idea for the common school had altruistic motives: he wanted a place for rich and poor to learn equally, without religious interests or ignorance, and be taught by well-trained, professional teachers. But ultimately the effect it had was to impose conformity. At the time there were no widely accepted teaching colleges, so Mann also popularized the "normal school" (no, really), which basically taught people how to become teachers and how to create mass-produced, obedient students. This normal-school system was powerful because the teachers effectively programmed the students with whatever the teaching materials told them to, and the governing bodies that wrote the teaching materials were very influenced by the economic upswing of the Industrial Revolution.

The rows of tables, the classroom style, the standardized tests, the universal teaching materials—all were made on the model of factory work, where, if someone didn't show up to work, someone else could simply be put in that person's place, like a cog in a machine. And this is how learning in school became as well. Everyone learned the same stuff, with very little room to budge, and everyone got graded on how much they could memorize. Everyone got "processed," churned in and out the exact same way. The underlying philosophy went something like this:

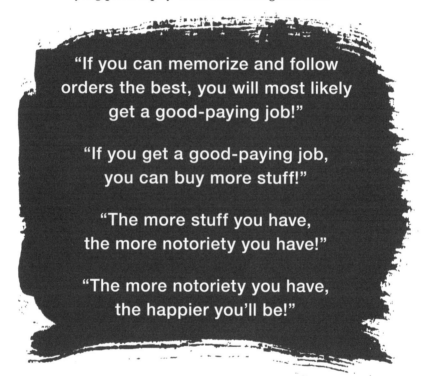

"If you can memorize and follow orders the best, you will most likely get a good-paying job!"

"If you get a good-paying job, you can buy more stuff!"

"The more stuff you have, the more notoriety you have!"

"The more notoriety you have, the happier you'll be!"

And thus began the societal brainwashing (teaching us, "this is how it *is* in the world"). Isn't it ironic that the name of the school system was the "normal school"—a place to make kids more subservient and "normal" and better *factory workers*? The government and factory owners got to define what "normal" meant back then. Don't you think that their "normal" is a bit different from our "normal" today?

So let's fast-forward to today: (deep inhale) We get served Google ads and we impulsively and unconsciously buy more stuff that we don't need; we have so many friends on Facebook we can't remember all their names (yet we're lonelier than ever before); and thanks to this more-is-better consumerist brainwashing, on top of living a more cluttered life (which, by the way, puts the environment further on its knees), more people are in debt than ever before. (Exhale, followed by an empathetic sigh.)

INDOCTRINATION IS POWERFUL

"You need to buy a house with a backyard for Hiro to play in, Miki."

Andrew, my parents, and I sat down for brunch in Williamsburg, Brooklyn, and immediately my dad and I got into a debate. My mom and Andrew eyed each other and settled into their seats, getting ready for the standard foreign-born-baby-boomer-father-versus-first-generation-immigrant-millennial-daughter battle.

"Why, Pops?" I looked at him with steady eyes.

"So you can start building toward your future! Now that you have a family, you need to become a responsible adult and buy a house." He said this with complete certainty.

"So I can put more stuff in it?" I break the fourth wall and wink (at you).

"No, so you can build memories."

"Can you please explain further, Daddy?"

"Think about our house. Think about all our amazing memories there: Agra-Palooza, Easter egg hunts, all the sleepovers with your friends, your birthday parties with our made-up games, ping-pong tournaments, pool party barbecues, volleyball, Jacuzzi nights, basketball, snowball fights. Do you remember the big house and some of the problems maintaining it, or do you remember the great times we shared in it?"

As he spoke, all those memories came rushing back, and I felt goosebumps run across my body. In that moment I totally understood where he was coming from and why *he* wanted a big house.

I *still* challenged him.

"I love all those memories, Daddy. AND, right now, I live in an awesome building in Brooklyn on the same floor as my close friends; Radha only lives five blocks away; and I love being with my community. It's so much better to me than living in a big house with just us and having to buy one of everything just for ourselves. It doesn't make sense to keep a house for only a few parties a year . . . Can't we make memories anywhere we go? Is it about the house, or is it about what WE created there?"

"I think you need a place to accommodate these memories. Are you suggesting we rent a venue to hold all our parties? Also, where will your kid play then?"

"We do have parties all the time, and sometimes we include our neighbors on our floor because they're our close friends, so we can have a big 'block party' on one floor of our apartment building. Also, the park is only three blocks away."

"So you think you'll go to the park three blocks away every day? You need a backyard!"

"Daddy, it's not like I have to get in a car—it's a two-minute walk."

Andrew jumped in: "Mr. A, our ethos about parenting is that if we love our lives and love each other, it'll be hard to raise an unhappy kid. Also, our generation is redefining ownership. You no longer need to own things when you can share stuff. So instead of owning things like a backyard and a pool and a snowblower, we share those things with the people in our community. This also gives us much greater flexibility to move around, travel, and have adventures, which are the most important things to us." (Think Airbnb, Uber, and other sharing economies that are crushing it for this very reason.) "It just doesn't seem to make sense in today's times to own a big house when so much can be done virtually now and the sharing economy is much easier to apply to our lives."

Society's pressure on us to "own our own home" clashes with our growing desire to see the world, remain fluid, and not be bogged down by *stuff*. My dad made a lot of sense when it came to building memories in a safe, known space, but since the Internet now grants us permission to explore every corner of the planet, seeing those places with our own eyes seems a lot more fun than having to spend a big chunk of our lifetime in one place, paying for a house and stuff in the house, constantly cleaning and maintaining it all, storing it, and guarding it. Why so much effort for inanimate objects when "home" is really where the people are?

"Okay, honey, you're right, different generations value different things."

Did my baby boomer immigrant Indian father just tell *me* I'm *right*? Wow, he *was* softening up as he aged.

While my dad was debating with me about "settling down" and buying a house, I thought about his current situation. After my parents retired, they sold their big house in Connecticut, got rid of 99 percent of their "stuff," and moved into a lovely, petite townhouse in West Palm Beach in a golfing community, where their veranda overlooks the second tee on a gorgeous, manicured golf course. And I have to tell you, I have NEVER, EVER seen them happier. They both are in the best shape of their lives; they have a great community of friends that they spend time with; and they spend months at a time living and adventuring in different parts of the world. They no longer have to worry about managing their stuff and dealing with a leak in the roof or "opening up the pool" or "winterizing the house" or mowing the lawn like they had in Montreal and Connecticut for 30-plus years. They simply pay dues to the community, who take care of all that. (Well, looky here, they're participating in the sharing economy too!) My parents are now both volunteering and writing books and having an absolute BALL.

It was interesting that my dad resorted to his "old-school" thinking by telling *me* I needed to buy a house now that I have a kid, when *he himself* has proven to be clearly SO much happier now in his late 60s than ever before, with a lighter life and 99 percent less nonessential stuff.

As I think about my own son, Hiro, I approach the concept of home ownership very differently than my parents. I'm not actually opposed to buying a home if it's treated as a community gathering space. But if we are able to live anywhere and give our kids more worldly experiences throughout their lives, without the burden of a big house that needs a lot of stuff in it, its maintenance, and the need to use it since we're paying a mortgage on it, I think Hiro would much prefer the adventure over having a big house with a lot of stuff in it.

"MY STUFF IS NOT MY LEGACY"

"Why did you decide to sell all your stuff and live by different bodies of water all around the world?"

I sat down with Andrew's mom, Sam, who decided to go for it last year, at the tender age of 65—to sell all her belongings and commit to adventuring for an indefinite amount of time. As a writer she found that water put her in state of flow, and it made sense to be around this natural element that made her feel most creative.

"My stuff is not my legacy. I spent my lifetime paying for stuff, cleaning stuff, storing stuff, and I was even conditioned to think that my kids would want my stuff—and now they don't want any of it. So what's the point of having anything at all?"

"How did people wrapped up in today's societal thinking react to you getting rid of your house and selling everything?" I asked her with curiosity. I assumed the words "gypsy" and "hippie" would be uttered somewhere in there.

But instead she said: "Almost everyone I talk with wishes they could do it and follows up with reasons they can't. Sometimes it's because they have people counting on them 'here,' or because they don't have the money, or they're not brave or confident enough. Sometimes it's because they don't want to do it by themselves, and sometimes they tell themselves they will do it someday. Or sometimes they have 'too much stuff,' some of which is 'worth a lot,' and it will take years to get rid of it all. To all that, I share Paulo Coelho's wisdom: 'One day you're going to wake up and there won't be any time left to do the things you've always wanted to do.' People don't have to quit their jobs or win the lottery or walk away from their responsibilities to live exactly the way they want to live."

She followed up with this: "But if there is any judgment at all, it's usually things like: 'She's at a certain age in her life so she can take her job anywhere. She's not taking care of two parents who are sick. She must have plenty of money in the bank.' Some of those are true, but not all. I certainly don't have plenty of money in the bank. When it comes to the stuff in my house, here's how I handled the things that had sentimental value: For example, I had a bookshelf full of books that I helped people write. Instead of keeping the books that had lovely personalized notes in them to me from the authors, I spent a few hours putting a video together, going over every book and sharing my thoughts and feelings about each one. I then gave the books to the library so they could be alive. I believe that if stuff can give life, it has a life."

DO IT NOW!

We absolutely do NOT need to wait till we're 65 to live exactly how we want to live. For example, I originally thought that I couldn't go anywhere because all my businesses were in New York City and I *needed* to be there. I made up stories like "my teams wouldn't be as *productive* without me" or "I *have to be there* or everything will fall apart." Not true. In fact my businesses are doing *better* without me running the day-to-day, because I set things up in a way that worked for me. I hired only self-starters (people who bounce out of bed with their own ideas and excitement to tackle the day and without attitude problems). I set up weekly calls with my team and make the calls sacred (so no missing them). I get weekly reports from my team on KPIs (key performance indicators) and marketing, PR, operations, creative, and finance updates from the previous week so we can go through them together, analyze the prior week, and see where we can create more efficiencies, making them feel like true co-owners of the business who hold each other accountable. I set the big vision and bring in the best people to execute it.

I can do most things virtually now, so I can travel and see the world if I want to. I don't feel pressured to buy a "bigger place" to just have something "new" in my life. We are so predictable—we get a new place or a bigger place just so we can have new stuff to look at and different stuff to focus our attention on. We have to ask ourselves, is this the life we want? A life where we move around and put different stuff in new, bigger places?

Of course, timing is everything too. In my twenties and early thirties, I was *also* learning so much in New York City that it was enough for me to stay in one place. My first business was a restaurant, so yeah, I couldn't really leave anyway, and I didn't create proper systems early on to give me the space to travel. I *also* wanted to plant roots and build a community in a magical place like New York City. But that was something I *wanted* to do, not something I *had* to do.

Society's obvious brainwashing to get us to *want* more stuff doesn't make a lot of sense anymore when all stuff does is bog us down. The last thing Sam said really resonated with me: "if stuff can give life, it has a life." There is no point in having an apartment or house full of stuff that is **not being used** when it can serve better elsewhere—like books serve better in a library than collecting dust in your living room, letting you show people how smart you are.

KEEPING STUFF ALIVE

"Indian Giver." You know the expression that is used when you give a gift to someone and then you take it back from them? It's meant to be shaming in nature, but if you knew the actual story, you'd want to rename this term too.

The story goes as follows:

In the 1700s (why do people rarely question stuff that has been "defined" in the 1700s!?) the Indians living in Massachusetts had a beautiful ritual. When members of the tribes visited each other, they would share a pipe of tobacco. This pipe was usually a beautifully crafted wooden ornament, and it would act as a peace offering between local tribes. When the visitor left, he would take the pipe with him. This pipe would get circulated among the tribes this way, staying in each tribe's lodge for a period of time and then getting passed around when visitors came.

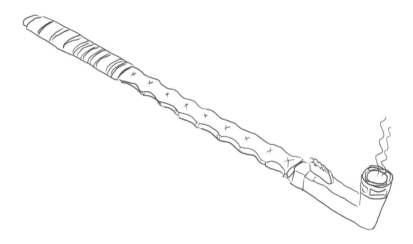

One day an English settler came to an Indian lodge and the tribe, in an effort to uphold the tradition, gave the Englishman the pipe. The Englishman took it home, and rather than continuing the tradition, just kept it in his house on his mantelpiece and never circulated it. Some time passed, and then an Indian tribe leader went to the Englishman's house for a visit. The Indian saw the pipe, and as the ritual goes, expected to share a smoke and take the pipe with him, so he did. The Englishman became so angry that the Indian took "his" pipe that he coined the term "Indian giver."

Pretty f**ed-up term, right? It's probably a good time to stop using that expression.

The point of this story is that stuff, when not circulated or used, is basically dead. It's a thing that's collecting cobwebs that you now have to deal with. That isn't fun, is it?

Wouldn't it be way more fun to keep stuff circulating and alive if you're not using it?

Society claims that to possess more stuff is to be great, and the more wealth people have, the more they believe it's their right to be ranked higher in the world and that wealth is an attribute of personal virtue.

Lewis Hyde, in his book *The Gift*, called bullshit on that notion. He quotes early 20th-century anthropologist Bronislaw Malinowski's description of a Pacific island tribe: "The important point is that with them to possess is to give." Malinowski praised the tribe's ability to give and to circulate things without claiming ownership. He said, "A [wo]man who owns a thing is naturally expected to share it, to distribute it, to be its trustee and dispenser."[1]

Imagine if the more wealth we had, the more we gave? I applaud people like Manoj Bhargava (founder of 5-hour Energy), who is giving away 90 percent of his wealth to charity. Bhargava's foundation is also trying to reduce fossil fuel emissions by 50 percent and clean the atmosphere of harmful chemicals from coal. He gets that when he ends up in a box with a billion dollars around him, he'll still be dead, so he may as well circulate his wealth while he's still around.

TIME TO PRACTICE ADDITION BY SUBTRACTION

I read the book *The Life-Changing Magic of Tidying Up: The Japanese Art of Decluttering and Organizing* by Marie Kondo. It's based on the Japanese minimalism philosophy that "less is more" and says to carefully examine each one of the possessions in your home (down to the old dental floss in your bathroom cupboard) and ask yourself, "Does this bring me joy?" If the answer is no, then thank those possessions lovingly for their service and kindly remove them from your life. As women we often love to keep things for "sentimental" value, but this is the time to officially give yourself permission to **CLEAN HOUSE!**

Once you declutter your house, do this with the people in your life too. Start inspecting them. Do they bring you joy or bring you down? Just because they've been in your life for years, it doesn't mean they're friends that add value to your life anymore (like, it used to be so much fun to gossip about high school friends—but you're over it now). Do a real assessment and choose only the relationships that bring you joy, lift your spirit, and challenge you to be better. Stop hanging out with people who just want to talk about other people.

The same goes for work. Just because you've worked with an employee or employer for a while, that doesn't mean it's meant to be. Does your job bring you fulfillment? Does the work you do bring you joy? Do the people you work with bring you joy? If not, you know it's time to gently move them away from the company (if you're the employer) or look for a new opportunity (if you're the employee).

The idea of practicing addition by subtraction simply means decluttering, releasing, and resetting your entire being, first with the actual physical stuff in your home (and storage unit if you have one—be honest, when was the last time you really needed anything in there?), then with the people and stuff in your personal life, and then with your work life.

FOUR PHASES OF THE RELEASE PROCESS (HINT: IT'S LIKE YOUR PERIOD)

Since I'm in the business of the nether regions, I figure it's the perfect time to draw a link between a woman's menstrual cycle and the release process.

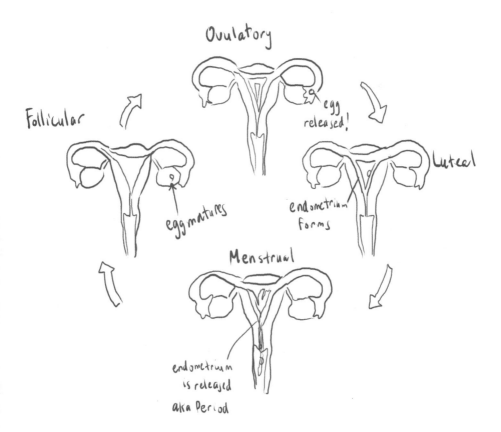

There are four phases of a woman's period: shed (menstrual phase), grow (follicular phase), drop (ovulatory phase), and float (luteal phase). We live in an endless cycle of shedding the old, growing and maturing as humans, dropping further into our own truth, and then floating in a world we want to actualize for ourselves. And then rinse and repeat. The goal is to get closer and closer to being fully who we are, unapologetically and fully expressed, with every cycle. The less stuff we have holding us back, the more time we have to express ourselves fully and authentically.

TURN RELEASE INTO A CEREMONY

This past New Year's, I finally mustered up the courage to do a three-day meditation ceremony. I had been told by so many friends that it was hard work, intense, and sometimes involved physical pain, and yet was life changing. I had heard of positive experiences ("Everything became so clear") and negative ones ("We got divorced after the ceremony," which basically means "everything became so clear that we should not be together"), and I was afraid of what would come up. Deep-seated issues with my family? Anger from business experiences? Pain from past relationships? The unknown was what terrified me. I wasn't ready for the longest time, and I kept kicking the idea farther down the road. Finally the stars aligned so that four best friends were going to do the ceremony with a trusted expert who had been practicing this facilitation work for well over a decade. It finally felt right.

I won't go into all the details of the experience, but I released SO much over those three days. I wept for hours over those who had hurt me and those I had hurt; I thanked, apologized to, and forgave in my heart those I had unfinished business with; I faced my immigrant scarcity mind-set and replaced it with abundance; and I had a full-body release.

WITH THE RELEASE CAME INCREDIBLE LIGHTNESS AND CLARITY. THE LESS MENTALLY BOGGED DOWN I BECAME WITH GRUDGES, HURT, PAIN, NOT-SO-GOOD STORIES IN MY HEAD, MORE SPACE I CREATED FOR NEW AND EXCITING THINGS TO EMERGE.

Releasing things through a ritualistic ceremony is an excellent way to move through these feelings, as we'll all inevitably go through challenging times at some point in our lives.

This is a great time to release all the stuff that's holding you back. You don't need to do a meditation retreat, but the point is to create intentionality around the release. True lightness and space will follow.

PUTTING IT ALL TOGETHER

"Stuff" (things we don't need, people who drain us, and work that doesn't bring us joy) has taken over a big part of our lives and consumes so much of our energy.

To be free is to have the space to go after what you want and not have "stuff" run your life.

Freedom and stuff do not go together in the same sentence.

In order to be a Disrupt-Her, you must (1) get back to your childlike state of curiosity, playfulness, and awe, and (2) intentionally release all the shit that's holding you back and bogging you down. The more you release, the more space you will create to invite in the things you DO actually want: new, awesome life experiences, deepening relationships, more time to do the things that light you up, more time to challenge the status quo on issues you care about, HAVING FUN, and being a badass in this short life.

DISRUPTION #2

EXERCISES

1. Take the time to go into each room in your home and declutter and organize carefully, keeping only things that bring you joy. You'll see how different you feel after you remove and release everything you don't need or want.

2. Do the same for your friendships. Write down the reasons that each close person in your life brings you joy and adds positive value to your life. You might be surprised that some people don't bring you any joy at all and yet you still spend time with them. Start to take notice of how you feel when you're with them and how you feel after you leave them. Energized? Tired? Feel through it. Once you're truly aware of how heavy certain friendships make you feel, you'll naturally let them drop away.

3. What are the three physical things or values that are the most important to you and why? Write them down and put this list in a place where you can see it daily. As for the rest of the things you busy yourself with, assess if YOU really need to do them or if you can delegate them.

RB ACCOUNTABILIBUDDY
ACTION #2!

LET YOURSELF HAVE FUN WITH THIS!
THIS IS A TEST TO SEE HOW MUCH
YOU CAN RELEASE!

TO HELP YOU RELEASE SHIT
THAT'S BOGGING YOU DOWN,
RB IS ASKING YOU
TO TAKE THE FOLLOWING ACTION:

EVERY TIME YOU FEEL YOURSELF
ADDING MORE CLUTTER TO YOUR LIFE—
THINGS YOU DON'T NEED OR PEOPLE
YOU DON'T ENJOY OR MORE
WORK THAT BRINGS YOU DOWN — DO THIS:

WAVE YOUR HAND UP AND DOWN
IN FRONT OF YOUR FACE SO YOU CAN

CLEAR

YOUR SPACE

AND DECLUTTER

YOUR MIND.

"STUFF" CAN BUILD UP FAST, SO BE
INTENTIONAL
WITH EVERYTHING YOU INVITE IN!

DISRUPTION #3

We need to follow a "career path."

We can follow a "lit path" where the dots of our life will inevitably connect.

*If you don't take the time to
think about and analyze your life,
you'll never realize that all of the dots
are connected.*

BEYONCÉ

MY DOTS

- 1999–2001: Unpaid summer intern at a film production company + random jobs to make $$ during college summers

- 2001–2002: Investment banking analyst

- 2002–2003: Semipro soccer player

- 2002–2005: Television commercial production assistant to producer.

- 2005–present: Founder of gluten-free pizza concept WILD*

- 2013: Wrote the book *Do Cool Sh*t*

- 2011–2017: Co-founder and C.E.O. of period-proof underwear brand THINX**

- 2015–present: International DJ duo Me2Me2 ("international" is a loose term, lol)

- 2014–present: Founder of modern bidet company TUSHY***

- 2017–present: Founder of Tinker Labs creativity and invention shop

- 2018: Author of book *Disrupt-Her*

* Brought in a fantastic restaurateur partner in 2013 to run the restaurants and give me space to start my next company.

** Came up with the idea in 2005 at a family barbecue, started working on the underwear technology in 2011 with co-founders, launched the company in 2014, transitioned out as C.E.O. in 2017.

*** Started working on TUSHY in 2014 but officially launched the company in 2016.

(The point of the asterisks is to show you that I wasn't running all of it at the same time, and I brought in teams to run each business before starting the next. You can't really focus on more than one project at a time if you don't have teams to work with you on each one, important to state that distinction.)

HOW I CONNECTED THE DOTS

The above seems like a spazzy career path by "society's standards," no?

But if you dissect the learning from each one "looking backward," they all fit together like perfect puzzle pieces.

- My unpaid summer internship taught me to "put in the sweat" to pursue my passions. My job was to read scripts, and it was during this internship that I learned the deep importance of storytelling, which served me immeasurably when I started my entrepreneurial endeavors.

- The random jobs I had every summer helped me make my $2,000 "parental quota." My parents gave me permission to intern anywhere I wanted as long I figured out how to make $2,000 every summer to contribute to my college tuition. This experience taught me to value and manage my time and money well. Time management is a key ingredient in succeeding as an entrepreneur or as a professional.

- Investment banking, as much as I loooooved to hate it, gave me a crash course in finance, which later really came in handy when I needed to put together financial models to raise money for my businesses, and it gave me credibility with investors, showing them that I could handle money. The long hours also prepared me for the long hours of entrepreneurship.

- Also important to note: I started my investment banking job across the street from the World Trade Center ten days before 9/11—when I slept through my alarm and missed the whole thing. This life-and-death experience eventually propelled me to leave banking and pursue my dreams with a deep sense of urgency.

- Playing soccer for the NY Magic taught me discipline and repetition, repetition, repetition to get a task right. Tearing my ACL three times thereafter taught me that excruciating pain was transmutable to strength and grit.

- My time in television commercial production—where I started out as a production assistant (picking up trash on the streets and getting directors coffee) and ended up producing commercials and music videos—taught me how to solve problems creatively on the fly.

All the above dots helped me become an entrepreneur. And of course, in starting each business, the previous business informed the next.

In 2005, at age 26, I started my very own gluten-free, farm-to-table pizza concept when nobody was talking about alternative health foods in a mainstream way. I was prepared for the hard, long restaurant hours because I gained the work ethic from working long investment banking and film production hours. I was able to do everything to make it work, from washing dishes to making pizzas to delivering them to doing whatever (even when some days felt futile and I had *so* many oven burns on my arms), because I had experience working every part of the job from my film production and soccer days. It was during this first entrepreneurial endeavor that I understood the meaning of endurance and how to "dig deeper" and "never, ever give up."

All the above experience and muscle memory gave me the ability to spend four years working on THINX for no money with my co-founders, creating the world's best period-proof underwear and building it into a real business, being on the front lines of breaking the period taboo.

All these years of experience, as winding as the path was, brought me to the top of the entrepreneurial game—and also taught me a lot about what *not* to do while building a business that had "hockey stick" growth. I learned how important it is to know who I am in every moment and receive all positive and negative experiences as opportunities to grow, no matter how challenging they are. I also learned how critical it is to have a strong, loving community around me during the harder times.

My newest companies, TUSHY and Tinker Labs, applied all the lessons and learnings of all my past work, including WILD and THINX. All experiences keep building on each other.

"CAREER PATH" DEFINED

As you can see, you don't need to have a traditionally linear "career path" in order to be fully lit up and be able to fulfill your adult responsibilities.

Society tells you that if you start in real estate, you should move up in real estate. If you start as a medical intern, you should move up to becoming an attending. If you start as an associate lawyer, you need to move up to become partner. If you start as an entrepreneur, you feel the pressure to stick with what you've started. Even Michael Jordan, quite possibly the best basketball player of all time, was ridiculed when he decided to become a baseball player after he retired from basketball. Society ate up *Michael Jordan* (!!!!), so clearly, following a linear career path has become the widely accepted way to go.

Let's examine this whole notion of a "CAREER PATH," two societally accepted words that many people follow blindly without questioning why our career needs to be something as linear as a path at all.

Dictionary.com defines "career" this way:

> An occupation or profession, especially one requiring special training, followed as one's lifework: *He sought a career as a lawyer.*

The key words to take from the definition are "special training" and "lifework."

Yes, doctors and lawyers require special training because there are unique skill sets attached to them (I wouldn't want to go under the knife with a surgeon who had been a poet the year prior, NO THANK YOU).

But as a result, careers that required special training influenced other career paths too—this method of "moving up the ladder" became the widely accepted way to progress professionally, and a single career track became your "lifework."

Society said: "Since people have to go through training to become real, practicing doctors and lawyers, we should probably make every career do the same thing: follow a very clear, linear path. We can easily wrap our heads around that, so let's just go with it."

Does that mean if you're a doctor, you can't switch? Or if you started out as a banker, lawyer, or consultant, and did that for a few years, you're stuck in that career? There is *still* a weird societal shame around switching careers after entering and staying in one field for a few years.

Society says:

"You failed at your last career, so you had to make a switch. *Tsk tsk.*" (#judgingsohard)

"You didn't know what path you wanted right away? You're immature for not knowing!"

"You're irresponsible and all over the place."

"You're quitting finance or real estate to become a chef? *Pffff.* What you really mean is you were fired, right?"

"You didn't succeed in this one thing. You must suck."

"Michael Jordan, stay in basketball. You're making a fool of yourself by doing anything else."

To that I say,
DISRUPT!

Training *is* important in becoming an expert in something. But what's important is not focusing on moving up the ladder and allowing the thing that you choose to do NOW define your life's work. You change over time as a human, so your love for what you do might change over time too—and that's okay! You're not a failure or irresponsible, you just want to live life as lit up as possible. You get that life on earth is short, so may it not be mundane!

Life shouldn't be defined by choosing a career path and sticking with it because that's what you chose early on. Career development is actually about deepening a skill set that you really want to get good at.

Becoming a better marketer, better artist, better creative, better problem solver, better designer, better architect, better finance person, better entrepreneur, better philanthropist— whatever you choose to "do" in your life must come from a place of real interest and curiosity to learn and grow in that area. If you love finance and moving up the ladder in finance is something that you actually enjoy, then that's great! Moving up the ladder in medicine is great if you love it! (But don't let your parents brainwash you into believing that you love it if you don't!)

When that yearning changes, it's equally okay to move on. Have faith that all the dots will connect when you look backward.

If you want to be an artist and your parents tell you to "get a real job," tell them that a "real job" is just an illusion of society. Who defines what a "real job" is anyway? Five years ago, "community manager" and "social media manager" were not jobs, and now they are. If the thing you love doing is paying your bills, shouldn't that be the most important thing to them? That's really what parents want at all costs for their kids: safety and security.

But is it really better to follow a safe career path or to choose something else? Perhaps a "lit path"?

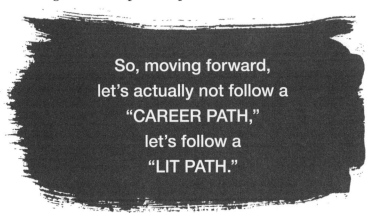

So, moving forward,
let's actually not follow a
"CAREER PATH,"
let's follow a
"LIT PATH."

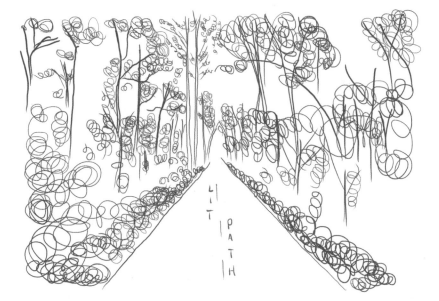

A LIT PATH LIGHTS YOU UP AND MAKES YOU EXCITED THROUGHOUT YOUR WORKING YEARS.

A LIT PATH GETS YOU OUT OF BED WITH A KEEN DESIRE TO LEARN, GROW, AND GET BETTER AT A SKILL SET.

A LIT PATH KEEPS YOU CURIOUS.

A LIT PATH SPARKS YOUR CREATIVITY.

Remember: There are often repetitive, tedious parts of every job; you have to learn to love these "wax on, wax off" motions too in order to get really good at something, even on your lit path.

A great example of someone following his lit path is Justin, who works at TUSHY with me. He went to the University of Pennsylvania for undergrad and Temple Law School and subsequently became a lawyer. He was first a tax lawyer and then moved to real estate law, and as time went on, he grew to really dislike the long hours, the lifestyle, and the work itself. Instead of sticking with this "career path" that was surely going to pay his bills and afford him a life of looking forward to weekends and vacation days, he discovered TUSHY online and sent me a cold e-mail. In his e-mail, he said that he had lived in

Japan for a couple of years and fallen in love with bidets, and he was excited to find a new company that was trying to bring this habit to America and disrupt an antiquated category. He offered to assist me for free to just help spread the "clean butt movement" that he was so passionate about. Over the next year, we agreed that he would work remotely in exchange for equity in the company. He would visit us from time to time from Philadelphia, where he was based. Every time he came to the New York office, I could feel his excitement to work on a passion project where he felt lit up and alive.

It took Justin two years to fully make the leap off the "safe-job-that-was-paying-down-his-expensive-student-loans" bridge so he could come work with TUSHY full time. He has since become such an invaluable member of this team that he earned the co-founder title after three years of working with the company. He lives in a beautiful apartment in the heart of the coolest neighborhood in Williamsburg, Brooklyn, and is thriving. Had he stayed on his linear career path—which so many people stay on because it's "safer that way" and "less embarrassing if things don't work out with the new thing," and most often out of fear of the unknown—he never would be living this lit-up life now. I know it can feel cliché to say "follow your light" when real-life stuff is involved, like paying down student loans or taking care of parents or not having any fallback plan to support your family, but all it took Justin was an e-mail offering to help out for free while he was still working responsibly. Only when he had a salary that made sense to him did he end up fully joining the team. Now he is a co-founder in the company, he has equity that is worth millions of dollars, and he is working for an organization and a mission that he is truly excited about.

Another cool thing is that Justin is also TUSHY's legal counsel, so his legal schooling has been very important for our young company!

Looking backward, everything makes sense; but when the future is still unwritten, we often stick with the original, safe plan of following a "career path." However, as Justin did so thoughtfully, you too must trust the light shining behind your eyes and choose THAT path. If you proactively do something to honor your lit path, in one way or another, it will inevitably work out.

PUTTING IT ALL TOGETHER

To be a Disrupt-Her, you must (1) get back to your childlike state of curiosity, playfulness, and awe; (2) practice addition by subtraction in all facets of your life; and (3) instead of a traditional "career path," find your LIT path based on your skills, things you are really good at and want to get better at. Diving deeper into your passions is the focus, not climbing the societally accepted career ladder.

STOP WHEN YOU GET TO THE ★
AND THEN SKIP TO THE NEXT NUMBER

***This connect-the-dots is from *Monkeying Around*.

DISRUPTION #3

EXERCISES

1. Get a notebook and write down answers to these questions: What skills do I have? What lights me up? What makes me come alive?

2. Connect your dots daily by writing down things that light you up each day. The more you write down every day, the more confident you will become in your lit path, the more your creative muscles will develop, and the more refined your ideas will be.

3. Do your research. Look for a business that's working on the thing you're passionate about and see if you can join them. Start by offering to help them for free! Learn what business models exist and then come up with your own if you can't find exactly what you're looking for.

RB ACCOUNTABILIBUDDY
ACTION #3!

WHO DOESN'T LOVE PUZZLES?!

**TO HELP YOU
CONNECT THE DOTS OF YOUR LIFE,
RB IS ASKING YOU
TO TAKE THE FOLLOWING ACTION:**

EVERY TIME YOU FEEL YOURSELF
WORRYING THAT YOU'RE
MAKING THE
WRONG CHOICE IN YOUR
"CAREER PATH," REMIND YOURSELF THAT
YOU ONLY HAVE 21,000 DAYS TO LIVE
OR LESS (UNLESS YOU'RE UNDER 22 YEARS
OLD, IN WHICH CASE YOU'RE SUPER ADVANCED),
AND WOULD RATHER CHOOSE
A LIT PATH.

CONNECT THE DOTS ON PAGE 76
AND SEE WHAT BEING LIT UP AND
CONTENT LOOKS LIKE!

DISRUPTION #4

Talking about money is tacky
(especially among women).

Money is flowing energy—the more
we talk about money as energy,
the more our energy around money
will shift too.

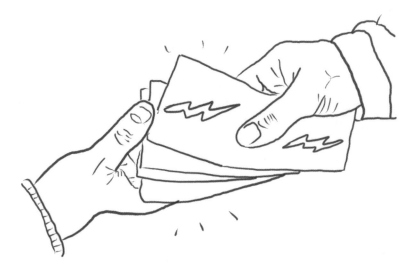

"Why does it feel like so many women are *still* so weird about money?" I asked Sallie.

"Like, we *still* hate talking about it. I feel like a hundred books have been written and a hundred companies have been launched to help women deal with money better, and yet it's still 'not okay' to talk about. What's up with that? But really, my bigger question is, why are we *so* risk averse when it comes to investing our money compared to men? It drives me nuts! Even as a start-up entrepreneur, quite possibly the riskiest field to get into, I too am super conservative when it comes to investing my own money. I had money just sitting in my savings account collecting dust for so long before I finally decided to invest it a couple of years ago, and now I'm kicking myself for not doing it sooner. Where does all this weirdness and fear come from?"

I was *clearly* very excited to ask badass Sallie Krawcheck all the questions I had bubbling up inside me when it came to money and investing. Krawcheck, founder of Ellevest (an investment platform for women) and formerly the president of the global wealth and investment management division of Bank of America, has been touted as "one of the most senior women on Wall Street"—so if anyone knew the answers to these questions, it would be her.

"Hormonal? Environmental? The way we're brought up?" Sallie mused. "It is true for most women, not just a few. The finance industry has done a poor job of addressing women's discomfort and talking us through the risk, mainly because men still run the finance world. It's still very much an old boys' club. Also, men value upside more than protection, until they lose their money and go apeshit. Women value downside protection seven times as much as upside."

My eyes grew wider. **Women value downside protection SEVEN TIMES as much as upside?** As I thought more about it, I realized that the finance industry is still run on a model that dates back to a time when women were mostly dependent on men's incomes. It's no wonder many working women still don't feel safe fully investing their money, because it hasn't been *that* long that we've had our own money to invest at all!

Sallie continued: "Women today keep 71 percent of their money in cash. That's double-digit percentage points more than men. We calculated that if a woman is earning $50,000 per year in her 20s and 30s, she has roughly $400,000 to $1 million of lifetime losses compared to a man because of her lack of investing. We're doing 120 percent of the hard work but end up retiring with two-thirds the amount of money as men."

That much in *lifetime losses* by simply not investing our money now?! Wow. I sat up straighter.

"Okay, so what should women who are not great at investing do to start?"

"You can start by putting 1 percent of every paycheck into an investment vehicle."

Some of you may be thinking, *Yeah, whatever, I live paycheck to paycheck already. I can't afford to put anything away.*

But let's actually think about this for a second. We're talkin' putting away $10 out of every $1,000. We can do that; we just need to make our own tea or coffee at home a couple of times per pay period instead of hitting Starbucks.

Let's say that $10 invested in the market earns 6 percent interest in a year; it becomes $10.60. Now, if the $10.60 earns 6 percent interest, that's another $0.64: $10.60 + $0.64 = $11.24. And now you're earning 6 percent on $11.24. And you keep going from there. That's how "compounding" works. If you hold your investment for many years, it becomes exponential.

This is super straightforward math; even my creative right-brained artist friends can do it. :-)

"Okay, but what if I make a mistake in my timing?" I asked. "Like, what if I invest when the stock market is up, and then the value goes down?"

Sallie reassured me, saying, "If you invest steadily, a bit every paycheck, it smooths out over time. Even with the crash of 1929, if you kept investing, you would have been covered in a few years. Automatically putting away only 1 percent out of each paycheck is easy to pull off. You don't see the money you're not making. The cost of waiting is *so much higher*. . . you are missing the power of compounding."

She passionately added: "I'm in the business of financial feminism. For example, one of the women I interviewed to come and work for Ellevest started to cry. I asked her, 'Why are you crying?' She told me that her grandma stayed in an abusive relationship with her grandpa because she had no money of her own and couldn't leave. This interviewee understood how important it is for women to have their own money."

Beyond Sallie's ability to make the topic of money mesmerizing, it was so refreshing to listen to a woman talk about it in such a powerful way. It became super clear that we all, but especially women, need to *get* money in a whole new way, in a truly empowering way, a way that energizes us.

Then it hit me.

What if we reframe money entirely and think about money as flowing energy itself? Energy is everywhere—it's our creative driving force, it flows from hand to hand to dream up all that is around us.

MONEY IS SIMPLY A MADE-UP ENERGY EXCHANGE IN A PHYSICAL FORM THAT HUMANS HAVE AGREED TO.

In today's society this physical "**money energy**" can flow in two directions. In one direction, **conscious money energy** is a positive exchange for our basic needs, like food, clothing, supporting our families and putting a roof over our heads, and keeping our communities clean and taken care of. Conscious money energy is an exchange that drives our passions forward and helps others drive their passions forward; it's one that allows our purpose to continue on.

In the other direction, **unconscious money energy** is a negative exchange for things like power, control, and greed; it fuels darkness like wars, businesses that seek profit at all costs, and corrupt governments. This negative exchange often comes from those who have had darker experiences in their lives, with scarcity in love, passion, and true connectedness. Nobody starts out wanting to go down the path of unconscious energy flow, which is why it's so important to remember what it was like to exist in a state of childlike curiosity, playfulness, and awe. If we can start from that place, we could reroute the unconscious money energy flow in a conscious direction.

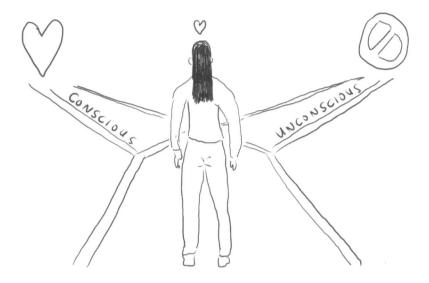

One meaningful way this metaphor can help us gain a new perspective is understanding that energy shouldn't just be stored for no reason; it must consciously be put to work to reap more energy. Otherwise it won't hit its potential. Same with money. We shouldn't just let it sit in a savings account collecting dust (although you should always have some rainy-day money available, like the *right* amount of stored energy to exist) but we need to invest money for it to reach its potential. In today's world there are plenty of investment vehicles (like Ellevest, E-trade, or Vanguard) that can pull money out of our bank account automatically and, rather than putting it into a savings account, put it into an investment vehicle that can grow and compound over time. Even people who have 401(k)s via their employers should consider investing some more of their money energy into these types of vehicles. Again, it can be as little as $10 a paycheck.

The more we understand money, our relationship to it, and how important it is to think of it as flowing energy, the more we will respect it and treat it with utmost love and care, which will inevitably create more of it.

A PENNY SAVED IS A PENNY EARNED

I grew up in a very Asian household where wasting money energy was a cardinal sin. We could buy necessary things, but wasting money? HELLLLL no.

I learned about the value of a dollar from the Value Tales book series that my parents read to me and my sisters when we were kids. One particular "value tale" was about Benjamin Franklin, one of my first inventor role models and the man who coined the phrase, "A penny saved is a penny earned." I still live by that today. It doesn't mean you're cheap; it just means you spend money thoughtfully and reasonably. I've been able to build the life I choose because I learned how to respect money energy and give myself enough energetic space to accomplish my goals.

So many people today claim we can't get by *and* save money *and* follow our passions at the same time. That just ain't true! We need to learn self-control, respect money energy, and live below our means. And you'll realize that you don't actually have to give anything up, because "stuff" won't matter to you anymore. Following your passions will.

BUDGETING

"Your allowance is $20. You spend $10 on stuff you need or want, and you're left with $10. That $10 you put away and save." Pretty straightforward, right?

When I was 11 years old, my parents taught me and my sisters how to budget and save. However, many parents in America don't teach their kids how to budget, because they themselves are burdened with credit card debt and have a lot of shame around money. But understanding how to budget is necessary knowledge that will last till our dying days, so it's good to learn as early as possible.

When I was 22 and just out of college, my twin sister, Radha, and I moved into a lovely $1,800/month basement townhouse on a gorgeous tree-lined street in Cobble Hill, Brooklyn. We were earning around $50K/year each and we were paying about $500/month in student loan debt. But we had to be careful with our money because we needed to pay down the loan, pay our rent and our monthly expenses, and still find a way to save so we could put that energy toward our passionate pursuits. I wanted to put away $500/month, every month. So I set up a savings account that automatically pulled the money out of my checking account. It was the best way to save that I knew of because I forgot that I ever had that money to begin with. I eventually got it to $750/month and it grew from there.

The thing that annoys me the most is that I didn't put that money in an *investment vehicle* that could have been earning and compounding interest the whole time. I let it collect nothing in a savings account, doing no more than keeping my original principal. But I did learn how to respect money energy early on, which still serves me to this day.

BEING FRUGAL IS NOT BEING "CHEAP," IT'S BEING SMART!

What I found out in the "how do I save?" game is that no matter where you live, there are always GREAT deals you can find. People say living in NYC requires a lot of money, but that's really not true! There is so much free energy buzzing all around us; it's all about how we harness it.

When Radha and I were living in Cobble Hill, Brooklyn, we found out that Cobble Hill Cinemas played new releases for $5 every Tuesday night.

We also discovered a gorgeous Thai place in Cobble Hill called Joya. The atmosphere was one of a nice sit-down restaurant with fresh flowers everywhere (you know a place is fancy when there are large vases of fresh flowers), but their food was super affordable and tasty. Their Tuesday specials included a pad thai that cost $7 for a heaping portion, so big that Radha and I could share it and still be stuffed. So every Tuesday night, we had a fabulous dinner at Joya for about $5 each ($7 plus tax and tip ÷ 2), and saw a newly released movie at the theater for $5 each. That's $10 each for a full night of wonderful energy in NYC! Clearly it's doable, you just have to find the energetic pockets.

These days in my neighborhood in Williamsburg, I often frequent "Taco Tuesdays" at a nearby (very nice) Mexican restaurant, ordering two delicious fresh fish tacos for $6. These tacos usually cost $12 each. These deals are EVERYWHERE in every city, you just have to look for them. Again, this doesn't mean you're cheap, it just means you're smart with your money.

Before you know it, you're saving real money energy every month, and it adds up fast. You just have to energetically release part of every paycheck for a few years and all of a sudden one day, you'll find a big pile of money energy sitting in an account, ready to be harnessed for your passions or for your family.

It's important to disrupt the money energy part of our lives as fast as possible because it's what will give us more ability to disrupt the rest of our lives faster. Money doesn't buy happiness, but it sure helps give us real energy to put toward the things we authentically want to get done.

INVESTING YOUR MONEY AND GETTING INVESTED IN ARE SIMILAR MINDFUCKS

Investing your own money and raising money for a business have similar mindfuck abilities. Both are incredibly intimidating, require a lot of energy to figure out, and are historically biased in favor of men.

"Why are you the right person to build this?" A male investor asked me.

Ugh . . . I mentally rolled my eyes. This would never happen to a man who had a solid business track record.

"Well, I literally *just* built a multimillion-dollar business in a similar e-commerce, direct-to-consumer physical product space, in a taboo category, so I kinda have an idea of what to do."

I was pitching my business TUSHY to a fund where all the partners were men . . . again. The stats are all too well known: only 7 percent of women sit in decision-making roles at investment funds and only 5 percent of women are getting invested in,[1] even though female-led companies are proven to be better performing than male-led ones.

I couldn't help but think of the gender bias called "Prove It Again!" A study was done by the Gender Bias Learning Project, and here's what they found:

In jobs historically held by men, men are presumed to be competent, while women often have to prove their competence over and over again. Thus men but not women may be given the benefit of the doubt. In addition, women's mistakes may be remembered forever while men's are soon forgotten. One of the most common examples of "Prove It Again!" is the double standard that men are judged on their potential, while women are judged strictly on what they already have accomplished.[2]

How annoying to manage this additional hurdle—but it did give me more fire to be even better and overcome this bias. I also didn't want to use it as an excuse, because I refuse to think that this notion is permanent, and I know that the energy around this bias is shifting. The more we reject and disrupt such "societal truths," the faster they will transform.

This experience with TUSHY also made me think about when my co-founders and I had to raise money for THINX for the first time too. It was damn near impossible initially because, again, pretty much all the investors that we met with were men. Think about trying to pitch period-proof underwear to conservative men.

"Uh, I need to show this product to my wife," was a common response.

"I doubt people will use this product. Seems gross."

"Should I be listening to this?" (accompanied by hysterical laughter)

So yeah, we didn't get any traction this way. After a solid six months of pitching the idea, no investor wanted to give us money to put toward the business, so we decided to put our energy into a Kickstarter campaign instead. We somehow scrounged together $65,000 on the crowdfunding platform, which helped us subsequently raise an angel round of funding to get us off the ground. Sometimes if energy doesn't come from one direction, we must try other directions to give it more space to flow in.

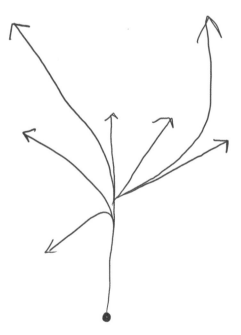

What has been clear to me when thinking about raising money from investors is that so many women *still* find it uncomfortable to talk about money, even for their own businesses. Women are known to raise just what they need (like I did) versus men, who raise exponentially greater amounts of capital, even if they don't need it.

If we can get past the weirdness of talking about money and remember that it's just a physical energy form, we'll be able to play with it in a whole new, fun, and different way—less serious and more fluid, respecting what it is and what it offers but with a new perspective around it.

This shift in perspective recently happened to my girlfriend Lara. She has been working in marketing for over a decade, and she put all her money into a savings account. She has been too intimidated to invest her money, mainly because her parents never invested theirs. Had she invested her money over the past decade, she would have more than doubled it, but instead she played it safe and didn't even talk about it with anyone. A month ago she was at my apartment with another girlfriend, Laurie, and all three of us started chatting about money for the first time. We've been friends for years, but this was the first time we really opened up to each other about how much money we had and where we were putting it. Lara admitted that she had not invested any of her money at all. After our open conversation about money, she was inspired to start learning more about investing and has since invested in cryptocurrency and opened a Vanguard account. She has already made thousands of dollars from her investments and wishes that she had opened herself up to these conversations earlier.

Disrupt-Hers are not afraid to talk about "tacky things" like money. Disrupt-Hers realize that the more we are able to treat money as energy and discuss it without feeling sheepish or tacky or dumb or generally uncomfortable, the more liberated we will be by it, the more fun we will have with it, and the smarter we will become about the energy transfer, and then we will be able to make better decisions moving forward.

PUTTING IT ALL TOGETHER

To be a Disrupt-Her, you must (1) get back to your childlike state of curiosity, playfulness, and awe; (2) practice addition by subtraction in all facets of your life; (3) figure out what your LIT path is as opposed to a traditional "career path"; and (4) recognize that money is a necessary energy source that gives fuel to your desires and passions and you have to be comfortable talking about it, saving it, and working with it. The more you can let your money work FOR you by investing it early on, the more freedom you will have to pursue your dreams. Truly, budgeting = freedom.

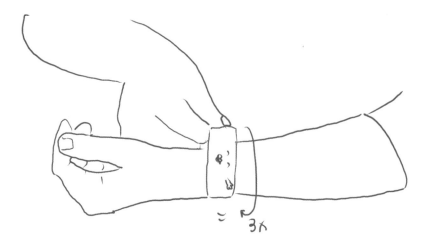

DISRUPTION #4

EXERCISES

1. Sit down, pull out your notebook, and create a budget. Figure out how much you're spending on a daily, weekly, and monthly basis. It's a good idea to use apps that let you see where all your money is and how much money you have in every one of your accounts.

2. Figure out what percentage of your money you can start putting to work. Start with 1 percent per paycheck—but if you can put more in, do it! Sign up for investment platforms like Ellevest (so you can put your capital to work and not let it collect dust in your savings account)!

3. If you decide to go the entrepreneurial route, it's so important to think about how you package your ideas to meet your investors where they are so they can "get it," especially during this time when men still dominate the money (for now). Know your audience. Use a data-driven approach with sound bites that investors can wrap their heads around.

RB ACCOUNTABILIBUDDY
ACTION #4!

EXCITED FOR THIS ONE?
C'MOOOON, GET EXCITED!
THIS IS ABOUT $$$!

TO HELP YOU GET CLEAR ABOUT WHAT
YOU ARE SPENDING YOUR MONEY ON,
RB IS ASKING YOU TO TAKE THE FOLLOWING ACTION:

REMEMBER JAFAR AND THE TRANCES HE COULD
PUT PEOPLE IN IN *ALADDIN*?

EVERY TIME YOU FIND YOURSELF IN ONE OF THESE
TRANCES ONLINE, WHERE YOU WANT TO
JUST CLICK 'N' BUY, DO THIS:

TWIRL RB THREE TIMES
AROUND YOUR WRIST WITH INTENTION.

AFTER THE THIRD TIME, ASK
YOURSELF "DO I REALLY NEED IT?"
IF YOUR ANSWER IS **NO,**
THEN **DON'T BUY IT**.

PUT THAT MONEY IN YOUR INVESTMENT
ACCOUNT AND WATCH IT GROW,   GROW,   GROW.

THE TWIRLING OF RB WILL BE A SYMBOL
OF THE UPWARD SPIRAL
OF YOUR MONEY COMPOUNDING AND WORKING FOR YOU
BECAUSE YOU'RE MAKING SMARTER DECISIONS

PRACTICE IT **NOW.**

DISRUPTION #5

Complaining is part of life.

Complaining is for procrastinators.
Instead of complaining about
what you don't like,
create what you would like.

"Ughhhh."

"What?"

"I can't believe X just did Y." (Insert name and action of your choosing.)

And then the chirping begins.

"*Chirp, chirp,* I can't believe it. *Chirp, chirp,* she totally saw it coming; *chirp, chirp,* that's so annoying, this always happens, *chirp, chirp* (insert other standard chirping)."

WE CLEARLY LOVE TO CHIRP

You know when you can't really see the hundreds of birds in a big tree, but the only thing you can hear is the loud, incessant chirping? That's basically what happens in our brain most of the time, unless we learn how to manage it. This chirping is the stories we want to gossip about, both internally to ourselves and externally to others; it's the constant internal dialogue we have about everything that has to do with everything; it's our sea of opinions, complaints, and judgments. (*He is right. She is wrong. Should I believe her or not? Do I agree or disagree with what she's saying? What's in it for me or them? Why would they do that? Is that true or false?*)

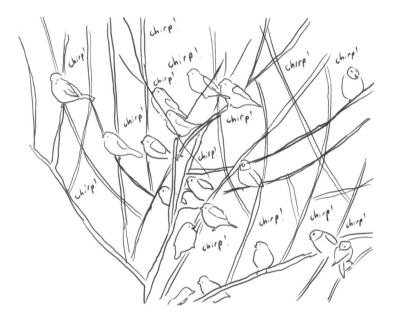

When we take that chirping outside our brain and into the world we live in, it often presents itself as gossip.

Anthropologists believe that throughout human history, gossip has been a way for us to bond with others—and sometimes it has been used as a tool to isolate those who aren't supporting the group.

A research group at the University of Amsterdam found that up to 90 percent of total office conversation qualifies as gossip,[1] and another research group, at Georgia Tech, found that gossip makes up 15 percent of e-mails.[2]

Humans have such a real fascination with other human experiences, and we often tend to focus on the negative.

You know when our lives are going great and the one thing that's going wrong is somehow the thing we think and talk about? If we post something thoughtful on social media, and 99 percent of the comments are positive and 1 percent is troll-y, we tend to focus on the trolls, right? Where does that come from?

It turns out that the human brain is actually built with a greater sensitivity to negative news. It's so automatic that it can be detected at the earliest stage of the brain's information processing. The reason we care so much about the negative stuff is because it's our instinctive reaction to keep us out of harm's way. From the beginning of human history, our very survival depended on our skill at dodging danger. The brain developed systems that would make it next to impossible for us *not* to notice danger, and thus (hopefully) respond to it.

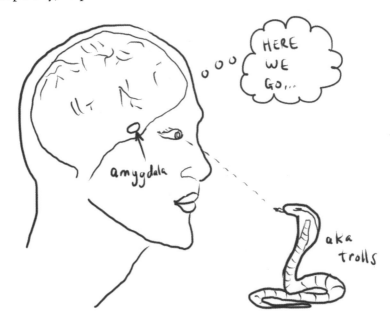

In today's society chirping is at its finest. Social media and the news media have learned how to use this fight-or-flight part of our brains (our amygdala) to their advantage by creating "click-bait" headlines. There are so many publications, blogs, and media outlets competing for our attention now; by creating inflamed, scary, or exaggerated headlines, they take advantage of the fact that human nature will make us click on them.

As people in leadership positions often are, I too have been on the receiving end of inflamed, exaggerated headlines. Rather than succumbing to the chirping and adding my own chirping to it, thus creating more chirping, I chose to take the higher road and look at the greater lesson. The greater lesson for me was to learn how to **react better** in tough situations and how to become a **Warrior Gatekeeper of my mind**, catching what I let into my thoughts and opting for constructive, productive thoughts instead of unnecessary, low-vibrational, unproductive chirping. (Less mean-spirited, negative chirping allowed into brain = happier life.)

Through this tough experience, I learned a lot about myself, learned to eliminate the negative chirping in my brain, and learned how to constructively look at where I *actually did* go wrong as a leader and how I can improve. I also learned a lot about what I am capable of enduring, which helps prepare me to continue down the path of creating and growing businesses in categories that are taboo in society.

MANAGING INTERNAL CHIRPING

My coach Lauren from Handel Group was my Mr. Miyagi. She held me accountable to my higher self through these tough experiences and showed me how to look for the greater lesson and not retaliate, even though my lower self wanted to fight back so badly while it was happening. I believe everyone needs an **ACCOUNTABILIBUDDY** (other than RB, of course, who is your subconscious's accountabilibuddy!) to talk things through with. This helps us organize our thoughts, especially when emotions are running wild. Lauren confirmed that these kinds of challenges will always arise for business leaders, and the sooner I can learn how to react better to them and catch the chirping before it enters my brain, the faster these issues will stop appearing as lessons I need to learn.

Lauren always turned challenging situations into games, which made it more fun for me to tackle them (who doesn't like games, even the hard ones?!), and she made light of all situations no matter how difficult they were.

Here's the game she gave me when it came to handling the negative chirping in my brain:

"Okay, so you're the Warrior Gatekeeper of your mind."

"What does that mean?"

"It means every thought that enters your brain has to get past your Warrior Gatekeeper."

"Got it."

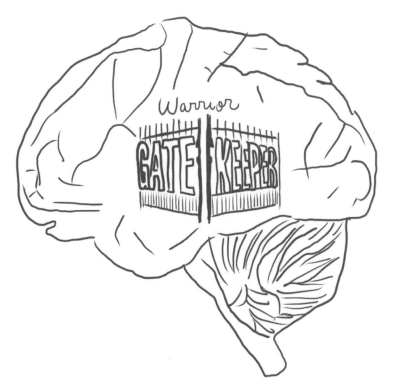

"Your game is to CATCH what comes to the gate and give it a name."

"A name?"

"Like this: 'Oh, there's Eeyore coming to the gate to mope and wallow about something like losing his tail, *wah, wah.*' Or 'There's Johnny Drama coming to the gate, trying to bring drama into my thoughts.' Or if a creepy person comes into your thoughts, tag them as 'the Creep.' Give each thought a name and tag them. Because every time you let any one of those things in, they take over your thoughts and then take over your body, and you can't think straight anymore because you've gone into a negative thought spiral; you're possessed like one of the White Walkers from *Game of Thrones.*"

"Right. And when you say 'catch,' do you mean notice the thought, like in meditation?"

"NO. *Noticing* is passive and almost defensive, whereas **catching** is far more proactive."

"Interesting."

"And then the minute you catch the thought, have fun with it, like '*Ha! Gotcha!*' or 'Really? That's what you were about to let in?' or 'Go away, not now.' And then if you actually *have* to deal with an issue, **organize it** and don't let it invade your thoughts whenever it wants."

"What do you mean by 'organize it'?"

"Like, 'That's a conversation I need to have only on Tuesdays at 11 A.M.' You're not allowed to think about it now or anytime except on Tuesdays at 11 A.M. with the appropriate parties. Then get rid of it in that moment and don't let it through the gate of your mind. And you're not allowed to let this topic enter your outward conversations—don't talk about it at all—until the allotted time."

Lauren added, "Oh, and there's one more thing. The Warrior Gatekeeper catches these thoughts with **love** and **humor**, not in a way that tries to make you feel bad or say that your life is out of control."

I totally got it. It was all about being fully present with every thought and catching each one before they entered the gate of my mind, which gave me full control of my emotional state. WOW.

So every time some negative experience popped up in my brain and I wanted to chirp about it, instead, I actually *got excited* because it flexed my Warrior Gatekeeper muscle, like a dumbbell would an arm muscle. I was excited to *practice* catching the negative thought with my Warrior Gatekeeper before it spiraled into a plan to seek retribution. These negative thoughts became a training ground for positive self-improvement, which then became an overall positive experience. We can always change our perspective and turn challenging experiences into positive ones.

TICK BITES DON'T NEED TO BECOME LYME DISEASE

Now that we've learned how to manage our "inner dialogue" and how to squash the negative thoughts that infect our own minds and bodies, it's time to move on to solving the "outward chirping." Let's think about outward chirping in the context of getting bitten by a tick. If I saw a tick on my body and started chirping about it (aka freaking the fuck out), by the time I got done chirping, this tick might have already burrowed its scary body into my body and caused real damage that could last a long time (like Lyme disease). But if I caught it right away and burned it off proactively (without outwardly complaining about it), it would immediately stop being an issue.

Outward chirping just delays the process of coming up with the solution. It's so easy to chirp about EVERYTHING these days, especially with a forum like the Internet, but how it is *really* constructive?

CHIRPING = PROCRASTINATING.

CHIRPING = DELAYING THE SOLUTION.

We often chirp about the things that are missing or not working in our lives. (I'm not making enough money. I hate my job. My sex life sucks. I can't find a guy I like. I'm not inspired by X friend that I see every week. I have no time to work out. I'm so stressed.) Or, in our new political reality, people seem to just chirp about "this policy changing" or "that initiative that I love getting defunded," and rather than calling their representative or starting a petition, people waste time chirping about it. Because it means they don't have to actually do something about it.

This has become a culturally accepted norm. We have come to believe that chirping about hating our job creates a shared feeling among people, that it builds community. But that's the wrong kind of community to build. Who actually wants a sense of belonging with annoyed, negative people? Chirping online is the same thing. It creates a false sense of togetherness against a common enemy: our job, "the man," the leaders of various governing bodies, your boss, a celebrity, etc. Somehow our culture made it such that if we chirp about these things, we're on the same team, but if we ENJOY them, we're ridiculed as "goody two-shoes" or "eager beavers."

For those who chirp all the time, each situation becomes an opportunity to find fault. Eventually this drains life of pleasure. Chronic chirping can also produce a negative mood state. The chronic chirper falls into a perpetual cycle of finding fault, feeling negative, and then being unable to face the next situation with an open mind. Eventually the capacity for feeling joy is compromised.

Yeah, nobody wants that.

SOLUTION? IF A NEGATIVE THOUGHT GETS PAST YOUR MENTAL GATE, THE NEXT BEST THING IS TO PRACTICE PATTERN INTERRUPT

"Whimper . . . "

"Whimperrrrr . . . "

"Wah!!!"

"Wahhhhh!!"

"Wahhhhhhhhh!!"

You know when a baby goes from a whimper to his hair standing on his head as he freaks out in a matter of seconds? I didn't fully appreciate this until I had my baby. It really does escalate quickly.

But let's be honest—we can all do that too as adults. We can spiral out of control really fast both in our minds and with others if we don't do something to stop it. This is where **practicing pattern interruption** comes in. When my baby goes into one of his tizzy fits, I change the scene, change his position, change hands (that is, give him to Andrew), rock him differently, and even jump in the shower with him when he really can't turn it off. Any one of these immediately calms him down; he can literally go from freaking out to smiling in milliseconds. I have just interrupted the pattern of his escalation.

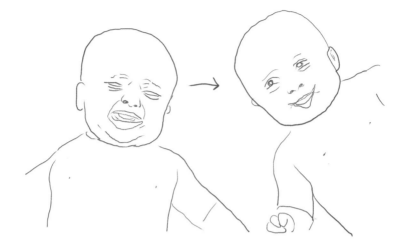

We're no different as adults. When we find our emotions escalating quickly and might do something we really regret, rather than letting the doom spiral take over, we can put ourselves in a different scene or position to practice pattern interruption. Sometimes that means taking a walk around the block, excusing ourselves from a conversation, or even something as small as going from sitting to standing up. Just doing those things can stop you from going apeshit, which will help your relationships and your own health exponentially.

"Yeah, but when I am in the middle of a heated conversation and someone tries to walk away from me, I get even MORE pissed. Like, 'Don't you walk away from me.' Or 'Don't you turn your back to me.' Or 'YOU are NOT getting the last word by walking out of here first.'"

Instead of just walking away, you might want to say:

"This isn't serving either of us *right now*. I'm going to go and take a quick walk and will be back when both of us are calmer."

Or:

"We've been friends for a long time. I'm going to go and take a break and would love to revisit this conversation tomorrow morning."

I've been there before, and it always works out better when I have the conversation in a calm state. So getting back to that calm place as fast as possible becomes the fun game to play, not the game of "winning the fight." Putting a timeline on when you will pick the conversation back up also really helps.

This doesn't just happen in conflict. Even when you're the only one complaining, you can go into a "complaint hole" and keep going and going and going until everyone around you is rolling their eyes. Catch yourself and practice pattern interruption by changing what you're doing right away.

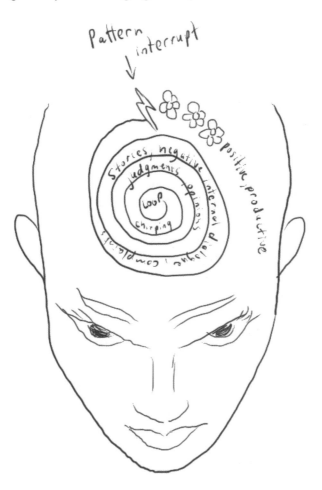

INSTEAD OF COMPLAINING ABOUT WHAT YOU DON'T LIKE, CREATE WHAT YOU WOULD LIKE

I learned at an early age that if there's something wrong around me, I can do something about it. There is no need to wait for the next guy or gal to solve it. There's nobody better than a couple of Asian immigrant parents to teach you that.

When I was growing up, my Indian father and Japanese mother moved their three girls to a suburb of Montreal. They had no family members in Canada and no social ties. And yet they quickly integrated themselves into the community. Regardless of their thick accents and meager resources, they managed to become organizers for things that mattered to them.

For example, when I was in elementary school, they couldn't find any academically minded summer camps in the neighborhood. There were regular summer camps and sports camps, but nothing that offered educational programs like anatomy, science, or math in addition to sports and recreation. Without any experience, my mom created the Gifted Children's Summer Camp, a first for our town, and it ran for more than 15 years.

Later, when my sisters and I were still in elementary school in Canada, my parents realized that electronics would be an important subject to learn and there wasn't a course that taught students about this. So my parents decided to start their own company, called Tomorrow's Professionals, and they created the first electronics course in our city for kids of all ages, teaching us how to build with breadboards, transistors, and resistors to make burglar alarms and run LED lights. They ended up selling their electronics kits and the program all over Canada. They had ZERO experience in any of this, but they figured it out.

My parents' way of existing really left a lasting impression on me. If there was a void in the world, we could do something to fill or fix it, regardless of money, contacts, or experience. All it takes is enough willpower and work ethic to get the thing done.

We actually have it much easier these days, because we can Google and YouTube anything and find a tutorial on how to set it up. It's amazing what's available to us now if we just spend a little time doing the legwork and not chirping about what's *not* working.

If you have a complaint to make to someone else, a good way to think about taking tangible action in that situation is to **come prepared with two to three solutions before making the complaint**. Making a complaint for the sake of bitching just isn't productive. Going to the boss with a solution for the problem is a much more positive interaction than just going into his or her office and complaining.

YOU WOULD BE A MUCH MORE VALUABLE ASSET TO ANY RELATIONSHIP IF YOU APPROACHED COMPLAINTS WITH REAL SOLUTIONS BEFORE BRINGING THEM UP.

RADICAL RESPONSIBILITY

When I read about a girl named Yusra Mardini and her journey, I was so inspired to **NEVER COMPLAIN ABOUT ANYTHING AGAIN**. It's one of those stories you'll keep coming back to when you get a blister on your ankle from your new shoes or have to pay a late fee on your phone bill or get an urge to complain about your paycheck. It's the perfect perspective check, and you'll see why.

Yusra is a Syrian refugee who fled war-torn Damascus. She was chosen to compete in the 100-meter butterfly and freestyle swimming at the 2016 Rio Olympics as one of 10 athletes on the Refugee Olympic Team. Here's her story:

Before Syria became unstable to the point that Yusra had to leave, she grew accustomed to training at swimming pools where the roofs had been blown off. She didn't complain about it; she was grateful to still find places to swim. Eventually she and her sister were forced to flee Syria, traveling through Lebanon and Turkey before attempting to get to Greece on a small dinghy. This boat was meant for six people, but it was carrying twenty. Within 30 minutes of taking off from Turkey, the boat's motor began to fail. Pretty much none of the people on the boat knew how to swim, so Yusra, her sister, and two men jumped into the freezing open waters and towed the boat themselves for THREE AND A HALF HOURS to the Greek shore. Did I mention that the water was FREEZING? After getting to Lesbos, a Greek island off the Turkish coast, Yusra and her sister traveled through Macedonia, Serbia, Hungary, and Austria before arriving at their final destination: Germany.

Yusra said after her trek, "It was really hard, for everyone, and I don't blame anyone if they cried. But sometimes you just have to move on."[3]

Dwelling—the opposite of moving on—is a killer, and I'll get into that in the next chapter.

When I think about people like Yusra or my parents, I feel even clearer that it's important to take real, tangible action to solve problems instead of only seeing what's wrong and complaining about it. They took **radical responsibility** to address their situations, no matter how challenging they were, without complaining about it. Radical responsibility simply means that no matter the circumstances or how difficult a situation might be, whether in or out of our control, we own it and do something to resolve it.

So the next time you find yourself in a real pickle or experience something that feels completely out of your control, the one thing you can do is take full ownership of how you respond. By taking radical responsibility instead of complaining, you get in control faster, which means you can move through the issue faster. You also end up learning a lot about yourself and are better prepared to respond to the issue the next time around.

COMPLAINING AND/OR CHIRPING ONLY DELAYS THE PROCESS OF DEALING WITH WHAT YOU HAVE TO DEAL WITH ANYWAY, SO WHY NOT SKIP THAT PART AND GET RIGHT TO DOING SOMETHING ABOUT IT?

It's important to note that it's okay to go through our individual process of healing—whether it consists of anger, grief, betrayal, sadness, or understanding and then gratitude. Somehow if we really sit with the hurt, gratitude always emerges in the end, and not just gratitude for what lessons emerge but gratitude for learning how strong we can be through a trying time. The most important thing I learned was to put a timeline on this process—for instance, "I will go through my healing process over the next two months and then come out on the other side stronger and braver." Without a timeline, some people can create an endless loop from a story of how wronged they were and not be able to move THROUGH it. I was able to move through my experiences because I honored the timeline of my process and had amazing people around me to help me through it. Now it's only occasionally that I get caught by a feeling of upset or sadness, but those moments are becoming more and more rare and are truly being replaced with a feeling of gratitude for what came from the hurt. Time is a brilliant healer too.

A Disrupt-Her will surely fall now and then in her journey, but she knows to expect that fully now and honor the process of feeling and moving through each hard time, taking radical responsibility for it, *not* chirping about it, organizing it, and deeply knowing that she will be more powerful because of it.

PUTTING IT ALL TOGETHER

To be a Disrupt-Her, you must (1) get back to your childlike state of curiosity, playfulness, and awe; (2) practice addition by subtraction in all facets of your life; (3) figure out what your LIT path is as opposed to a traditional "career path"; (4) start investing your money wisely; and (5) act as a Warrior Gatekeeper to your mind to stop the mental chirping and share tangible solutions before complaining about something.

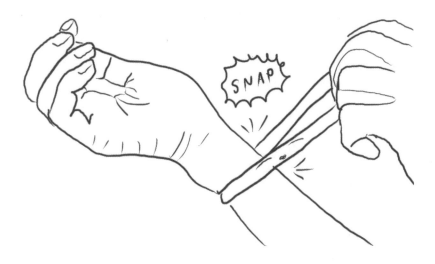

DISRUPTION #5

EXERCISES

1. Practice being a Warrior Gatekeeper of your mind. Every time a negative thought pops into your head and you want to chirp about it, inwardly or outwardly, catch it, name it, and organize it. You can absolutely train your brain like you would train any muscle in your body. You need to practice this daily—and have fun with it! When a negative thought appears in your mind, turn it on its head and get EXCITED to practice catching the thought. (RB will help you through this; you'll see how below.)

2. Practice pattern interruption when you do find yourself escalating quickly: change the scene, walk away from a conversation, or do something differently to get yourself out of your mental spiral.

   • If you see an issue in your community, don't just complain or wait for someone to take action; take tangible steps to do something about it. Start by writing the 5 Ws of who, what, when, where, and why for what you want to create. It will help crystallize a lot for you. Then, once you are clear, use the three Cs of solving problems in your community:

- CHECK (i.e., research) and see if a similar thing exists in a different community. If so, no need to reinvent the wheel—see if you can bring it to your community.

- If something like what you want doesn't exist anywhere, CONTACT the person you think would be in charge of such a thing if it existed. Be relentless in your outreach. If they don't respond after the first try, don't stop until they do. You need to hear a definitive NO before moving on to the third C.

- If nothing like what you want exists, or if the person you contacted said a big, fat, definitive NO to helping you, don't complain about it. CREATE a plan. Start finding people who want similar things by going to events, meet-ups, conferences, etc., with like-minded people. Nobody is going to come to you, so you need to be proactive.

3. Try to incorporate gratitude into your daily practice. Start with thinking of three things you're grateful for and three things you're looking forward to every morning, and watch how it helps improve your mood for the rest of the day.

4. Resist the urge to blame others. Take RADICAL RESPONSIBILITY for everything that has happened to you and focus on self-improvement and solving the problem in front of you instead of complaining about it. Taking radical responsibility actually gives you control back, and YOU can now focus on what YOU can do to move forward.

RB ACCOUNTABILIBUDDY
ACTION #5!

TRAINING OUR MIND
IS SUCH A FUN CHALLENGE,
ISN'T IT?

TO HELP YOU STOP THE CHIRPING
IN YOUR BRAIN, REMIND YOURSELF
THAT YOU ARE THE WARRIOR GATEKEEPER
OF YOUR MIND,
TO PRACTICE PATTERN INTERRUPTION
WHEN YOU DO FIND
YOURSELF SPIRALING,
AND TO TAKE RADICAL
RESPONSIBILITY
TO SOLVE PROBLEMS AROUND YOU
WITHOUT BLAMING OTHERS.
(THIS IS A LOT, I KNOW;
THIS IS WHAT IT TAKES TO BE A DISRUPT-HER!)
RB IS ASKING YOU TO TAKE THE
FOLLOWING ACTION:

EVERY TIME YOU FIND YOURSELF
COMPLAINING OR MENTALLY SPIRALING
OUT OF CONTROL,
SNAP RB HARD ON YOUR WRIST TO PRACTICE REAL,
PHYSICAL PATTERN INTERRUPTION.
IT SHOULD STING SO GOOD EVERY TIME
YOU DO IT SO YOU WILL BE REMINDED OF THIS
BEFORE IT HAPPENS AGAIN.

DISRUPTION #6

We have to be perfect
and not make mistakes.

It's not about "being perfect,"
it's the iterative process
that's perfect.

"Do I look fat?"

"No, you look great. Why are you asking? Is it because I look fat?"

The number of times my twin sister, Radha, and I have asked each other that in the past in various outfits is (not so) hilarious.

It should be a joke and even cliché at this point to talk about how shaming it is for society to tell women to look a certain way and act a certain way, because we are SO aware that this shaming is happening—but sadly it's STILL a thing. It's *still* a topic of conversation, because we are *still* somehow hammered with hundreds of media impressions daily that tell us what society deems "perfect."

WHAT IS "PERFECT" BY SOCIETY'S STANDARDS?

Still today the media suggests that "perfect" is tall and skinny with big boobs, small waist, and a big butt; perfectly coiffed voluminous hair, voluptuous lips, big eyes, tiny nose, and long eyelashes; clear, milky, smooth skin; perfectly fitted clothing; and a sweet laugh. Smart? Enough but not too threatening. Energetic? Not too much or it's unsexy. Cares about "world peace"? Bonus points. You might be thinking that we're past this, but it's still unfortunately true in many parts of the world, including America.

Have we made progress? Sure. Look at Ashley Graham. She's a real thing and was on the cover of *Sports Illustrated* as a plus-size model. Are STRONG women way more celebrated now? Absolutely. Serena Williams had a powerful cover on *Vanity Fair* magazine and owned her pregnant body 100 percent.

I too feel the shift happening around me. I was at spin class just the other day and I started tearing up in the middle of class because I had gone with a bunch of girlfriends, and five of them were lined up on bikes in front of me, and as we were pedaling our hearts out, I saw such powerful, fierce, competitive, supportive, and STRONG women. It never crossed my mind how "skinny" they looked; I was overwhelmed by their STRENGTH and POWER.

So yes, the paradigm is shifting to STRONG and POWERFUL versus "skinny and not too threatening," but there is still so much unraveling left to do in this society that has been wrapped up in the current patriarchal system for far too long.

WHY DO WOMEN FEEL THE NEED TO BE "PERFECT" PROFESSIONALLY?

It hasn't been that long since the majority of women were housewives, so the professional world is *still* getting used to seeing women in powerful business positions. And because many women are just starting to truly find their power, they are tentative about fully stepping into it without having "all t's crossed and i's dotted." They want things to be absolutely perfect before launching their "thing" or going for a bigger job.

Hewlett-Packard came out with an internal report stating that men apply for a job when they meet only 60 percent of the qualifications, but women apply only if they meet 100 percent of them.[1] Women feel the need to check all boxes and be a perfect fit for a role before they think they are ready to go for it.

THE GOAL HERE
IS TO DISRUPT THAT
"PERFECTION" NOTION
AND REALIZE IT'S
THE ITERATIVE PROCESS
THAT'S PERFECT.
IT'S ALL ABOUT LEARNING
AND IMPROVING AS WE GO.
THE PERFECTION IS IN
THE CONSTANT
IMPROVEMENT.

If we wait till we're *actually* perfect, which will never happen, nothing else will ever happen either.

"Look, I think it was a mistake that I applied for this job," she said to me.

I was sitting in my office, taking a call from a woman I was interviewing for a digital marketing job.

"Why is that?" I asked.

"Well, I think I overreached. I'm not sure I can handle such a role, based on the growth marketing challenge you sent me."

Before each employee gets hired, we have them complete written challenges to see how they think in the role they are applying for.

"Okay, what part are you unsure about exactly?"

"Well, the analysis of the numbers is something I can do in my sleep; it's just that for me to decide which direction the marketing should go for the whole company feels like it would be really daunting right now. I don't know if I'm ready to call the shots like that."

I stopped her from continuing, and with an encouraging tone, asked her:

"Do you think a man would ever say that, sitting in your seat right now? Or do you think he would say, 'Put me in, Coach' and then figure it out?"

She laughed. "Probably the latter."

"So what's stopping YOU from saying that too?"

She paused for a while before responding. Finally, she said: "Well, I guess in my last job, I was *so* bullied and made fun of by the guys that I lost all self-confidence."

I was incredibly surprised at her candor and proud of her for voicing that realization right away in this interview. I could feel the surprise in her voice too that she had said this out loud.

"Sorry, I shouldn't have said that." Her tone changed to shame.

"I'm SO glad you did; the more real you are, the more I can understand you. Also, knowing that, wouldn't you want to prove *to yourself* that you ARE good enough and capable enough to DO this?"

She paused again, longer. It was as though a switch had been flipped; I felt the energy shift. It felt like she sat up straighter in her chair on the other end of the line. A determined tone appeared in her voice.

"You're right. I AM capable. I CAN do this role. I WILL complete your marketing challenge and get it back to you, and I will knock it out of the park."

She didn't end up getting the job, mainly because we found a more fitting candidate for the position, but the point is that she wouldn't have even been a contender if she didn't actually believe in herself enough to even *attempt* to complete the challenge, because she was so traumatized by her previous job. Trying to be "perfect" in every aspect of a job is next to impossible, and if you feel the need to be perfect before moving forward, it will never happen.

Especially after a setback, the most important thing is to find the courage to put yourself back in the ring fully, with the Warrior Gatekeeper of your mind stopping the negative thoughts, rather than sitting on the sidelines and thinking that you're "not good enough anymore" but one day you "might be again." This woman wouldn't have learned anything by not making an attempt. You can't disrupt anything if you don't go for it fully at every turn.

Even after my own setbacks in my businesses, I could have been scared to go back out and go for it again, but I was grounded in my truth, I learned where I needed to improve, and I knew that the only person stopping me from living fully alive was me—so I kept going with *all of me.*

YET THE PRESSURE IS STILL ON TO BE PERFECT . . . OR ELSE

In specific male-dominated fields, women *especially* feel scrutinized, especially about their intellectual and physical capabilities. Imagine what it must be like for female fighter pilots.

"It was such a high-pressure experience for me," she said.

My dear friend Zach is a decorated Marine captain. One day at his place, I met a female fighter pilot from the Marine Corps.

"Why?"

"Because I'm a female fighter pilot in the Marine Corps, and there are so few of us around."

"And?"

"And so every time I make *any* mistake, like not landing the fighter plane *absolutely perfectly,* I let *my entire gender down.* All the male Marines around me say, 'See? This is why we don't let girls get behind the wheel.' And then they all start making fun of me incessantly, and I'll never live it down. It also further perpetuates the stereotype that 'girls can't drive' or 'girls can't fly.' And they say these things over and over to me. What's even more shitty about this is that I get extra nervous because of this gender stereotype and the constant scrutiny, so I end up messing up *more.* And it keeps spiraling until I have no self-confidence left. And then I have to really get centered and build myself back up. It's SO hard when all eyes are on you, when everyone is ready to pounce if you make one tiny wrong move."

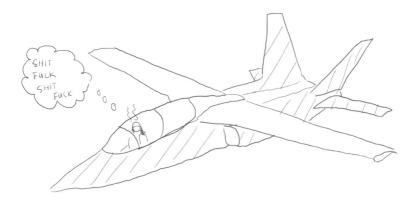

To be in a high-pressure situation (where men dominate the industry) *and* get made fun of on top of that would require a lot of mental strength to overcome. So it's even more important to use these situations as opportunities to practice being the Warrior Gatekeeper of our mind and catch the self-doubt that people around us are trying to shove inside us. This practice will in turn make us stronger, more resilient, and ready to continue down the path of disrupting the status quo.

FEMALE ENTREPRENEURS AND LEADERS ARE ALSO TOLD TO BE PERFECT . . . OR ELSE

In the entrepreneurial world, female entrepreneurs *still* aren't getting invested in nearly as much as men, because women are held to a different and higher standard.

I have been on the receiving end of this gender bias too, so I understand why it's so hard for women to *PRESS GO!* and launch something or create something, because any mistakes may be "remembered forever." Kind of a lot of pressure, wouldn't you say?

"PRESS GO!" DEFINED

PRESS GO! means
charging forward on the things
you want to create in the world,
both on your **LIT** path and overall in life.
PRESS GO! means getting after it fully
and unapologetically, understanding the risks
but still making it happen.

"Are you sure you want to talk about anal play with TUSHY when society is already ready to pounce on you?"

I laughed.

I knew that if I was going to fully PRESS GO! in taboo categories, I would be even more exposed to things potentially getting taken out of context, especially when talking about private parts like vaginas, buttholes, breasts, etc. I had to make the call and either really PRESS GO! and actually break taboos unapologetically or play it safe and not change culture at all. If society wants to make me out to be a "bad guy" to keep the status quo, that blowback is part of being a Disrupt-Her, and I have to learn to accept it.

I also realize that things *will* continue to get easier for women because data is emerging that female founders are outperforming male founders. In fact, according to First Round Capital, "startup teams with at least one female founder performed 63 percent better than all-male teams."[2]

(The goal here isn't to say that women are better than men; it's to show that women are more than equal contenders.)

Yet the message is still getting reinforced by society time and again that if we aren't "perfect" in every aspect of our lives, especially as women in leadership roles, then we could get killed in the media and by society.

The goal here is to catch ourselves before we perpetuate preconceived or societal gender biases and beliefs and instead attempt to be fully open to new possibilities.

ITERATION IS PERFECTION, STAGNATION IS DEATH

To repeat for emphasis, it's not at all about "being perfect"; it's the *iterative process that's perfect*, the process of making micro-iterations, small adjustments on ourselves, minor self-improvements ALL THE TIME, and not stopping, ever. Holding on to and staying in one state of being (like the notion that "I am perfect!") creates a stagnant experience.

BY PRACTICING CONSTANT SELF-INQUIRY AND MOVING FORWARD WITH SMALL POSITIVE ADJUSTMENTS, WE GAIN MORE AND MORE CONFIDENCE IN OURSELVES.

For example, when launching my companies, I found it was so important to listen to customer feedback and then collect all the feedback, figure out what the most frequent comments were, and improve the product based on this constructive feedback. The moment we think we're perfect and nothing needs to change is the moment things will inevitably go downhill. The companies that stand the test of time are the ones that continue to iterate and make adjustments constantly.

What do video rental stores, music stores, taxis, publishing companies, bookstores, newspapers, radio stations, landline phone companies, and retail stores have in common? They're not iterating fast enough. They're going out of business one by one.

Nearly 9 out of every 10 companies that were on the Fortune 500 list in 1955 were gone in 2016.[3] They didn't realize how important it was to keep making micro-adjustments and improvements as times changed.

In my businesses my teams know that my favorite saying is "Iteration is perfection." In fact it's one of our core values at my companies. We know that our designs, copy, marketing, online store, operations, etc., can always be better; we also know that it's important to start somewhere and then learn and make small positive adjustments rather than not start at all. So many people, women especially, talk themselves out of taking the first step just because they don't want to have to explain anything if it doesn't work out.

Our website has been an iterative process from day one. If we look at the "Wayback Machine" to see all eight iterations of our website, it's almost hilarious to compare where the website started and where it is now. With each new site developed and redesigned and optimized, I became prouder. But I was proud of the first site too (even if it was the ugliest thing ever), because it was a starting point and we could only go up from there. We just **didn't stop there**. See the distinction? We didn't ever remain stagnant and satisfied; we iterated our product designs, marketing strategies, brand, website. And all those small iterative adjustments over time took us from doing $25,000 a month to millions of dollars a month in revenue.

STAGNANT WATER PROMOTES PESTS

When you're in the restaurant business like I've been for 12 years, you know that stagnant water equals major fines by the health inspectors. This is because stagnant water promotes pests (roaches, rodents, etc.) and bacterial growth.

The same goes for your mind. If you stop working hard and moving in a forward direction, you stop the process of self-improvement, and worse, pesky thoughts start to come up. When you have nothing to do on a Saturday except let your mind wander to the shitty thing your sister said to you the other day, it doesn't help you in your quest to become the best version of yourself, does it?

Notice how the people with the most time on their hands are the ones with the most problems? The more you keep moving and improving, the faster you can move through problems. The moment you stop or give up is the moment that thing you care about dies too. It's important to take a beat and write down the things that DIDN'T go right and learn from them, but then keep movin', baby!

Women are much more prone to stagnation. This is because we were raised having to look perfect and be perfect, so when things don't work out, we are much harder on ourselves and feel embarrassed that we failed to be "perfect." Men can bounce back from failure much more quickly, because failure for men is almost like a battle scar to be proud of.

DWELLING IS SYNONYMOUS WITH STAGNANT WATER

Close your eyes.

Think of a clear, flowing river. Think of what it looks like, feels like. Picture the happy, healthy fish swimming and jumping in it.

Sit with that for a second.

Now think of a still pond. Think of the murky, dark edges with toads and flies, and the gunky lime-green buildup gathering on the borders of the pond.

This is how the mind works too. The flowing river is a healthy mind and the stagnant pond is a murky mind, one that's infected by negativity. Dwelling falls into the stagnant pond category, just like stagnant water in a restaurant.

It's so easy to dwell on things that don't go right.

Women often dwell more because of the "perfection obsession," and we must choose to move through experiences, both good and bad, like a flowing river. The more stagnant our thoughts are—the more we dwell—the more stuck we get.

I would say one of my better qualities is that I have a terrible memory for "negative" experiences—I somehow remember them all as positive learning experiences when looking back. I give myself permission to feel the experiences fully, but I don't dwell for too long.

Give yourself a time frame (say, up to two weeks) to feel your emotions fully, and then it's time to flow through the experience, like a healthy river.

I challenge you to remember even your most negative experiences fondly—because it means you learned, you grew, you iterated forward and understood a new lesson.

(By the way, did you find yourself judging me for talking about one of my "better qualities"? That's also patriarchal brainwashing, which taught women not to be confident but to "be humble"; and yet men are allowed to be confident. The Gender Bias Learning Project talks about how confident women are seen as "shameless self-promoters" while confident men "know their own worth."[4] I'm just sayin', catch your own biases.)

PUTTING IT ALL TOGETHER

To be a Disrupt-Her, you must (1) get back to your childlike state of curiosity, playfulness, and awe; (2) practice addition by subtraction in all facets of your life; (3) figure out what your LIT path is as opposed to a traditional "career path"; (4) start investing your money wisely; (5) become a Warrior Gatekeeper of your mind by actively catching what comes to your mental gate (and then practicing pattern interruption if you do accidentally let in a negative thought and start spiraling out of control); and (6) iterate and get better every day in all the things you're doing instead of focusing on being perfect.

DISRUPTION #6

EXERCISES

1. Whenever you feel like you're "not perfect," practice using the Warrior Gatekeeper of your mind to catch the thought and then name it something like "Brainwash Betty" (after society's brainwashing). And then laugh at it by saying, "Ha! Caught you, Brainwash Betty!"

2. Repeat the mantra "Iteration is perfect; stagnation is death" when you find yourself in your "perfection obsession." Practice making micro-adjustments every day. They add up quickly, and results follow.

3. Whenever you find yourself dwelling on something that's not serving you, if your Warrior Gatekeeper doesn't catch it first, visualize a flowing river and then let the thought float away. The more you can let go of your thoughts before they overtake your mind, the better.

RB ACCOUNTABILIBUDDY
ACTION #6!

BEING "PERFECT" DOESN'T LEAVE ROOM FOR A LOT OF FUN DOES IT?

IT'S TIME TO HAVE FUN
WITH THE PROCESS OF ITERATING FORWARD,
WHICH THEN HELPS YOUR COMMUNITY
AND SOCIETY ITERATE FORWARD TOO.
ITERATION IS PERFECTION; STAGNATION IS DEATH.
IT'S ALL ABOUT THE PROCESS OF CONSISTENTLY
MAKING MICRO-IMPROVEMENTS FOR YOURSELF
AND YOUR WORK. WHEN YOU DO THIS,
YOU WILL FIND FULFILLMENT.

WHENEVER YOU FEEL INSECURE
AND "NOT PERFECT"
OR LESSER THAN,
THEN GAZE AT YOURSELF
IN A MIRROR
FOR 60 SECONDS.

RB IS ASKING YOU
TO TAKE HER OFF AND
HOLD HER AROUND
YOUR RIGHT EYE,
TO REMEMBER THAT
YOU'RE DOING IT AND
THAT YOU LOVE THE PROCESS
OF ITERATING FORWARD.
WHEN YOU PUT
POSITIVE LOVING INTENTION IN
YOUR OWN GAZE, YOU WILL
DEVELOP A DEEPER SENSE OF LOVE
FOR YOURSELF TOO.

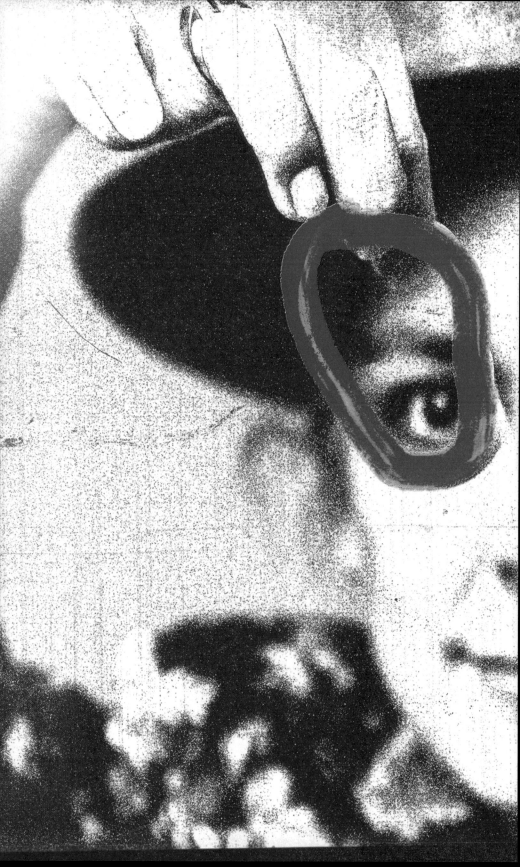

DISRUPTION #7

Haters gonna hate.
Once a hater, always a hater.

DISRUPTION

Hate-Hers exist within all of us.
The faster we catch ourselves
acting out as HATE-HERs,
the faster we can go back
to being LOVE-HERs.

"What do you mean, Jen lied?"

"I moved out because she was a shitty roommate—and then she started spreading rumors about me!"

My friend Lisa was distressed as she shared this with me.

"What happened?"

"She told everyone that *she* moved out because I came on to her boyfriend. REALLY!? It's a complete lie! And what's crazy is that she enlisted some people to jump on her bandwagon. It's really so petty and sad. She also accused me of saying things I never said and is bad-mouthing me to everyone online and to my friends too. In my head, I just say, 'Get a life and move on!' But she's intent on trying to mess with MY life. Initially I was upset and wanted to tell everyone the truth, but I decided against it because I just didn't want to be part of a nonsensical catfight that perpetuates girl-on-girl hate in the world. I really do just want to move on, but she won't let me. It's as though she has nothing better to do with her life."

Does this feel all too familiar to you?

"Well, this is clearly catty revenge to hurt you because you hurt her by moving out," I diagnosed.

"She is pretending to be the victim in the Drama Triangle, but she is actually the persecutor and trying to take me down to get back at me."

"What's this 'Drama Triangle'?" I asked.

"The Drama Triangle is the persecutor, the victim, and the rescuer. I've been reading up on this since all this stuff with Jen happened. It's pretty spot-on as it relates to what I experienced."

We'll get into the Drama Triangle later in this chapter.

I've been hearing more and more about "girl-on-girl" conflict and how girls and women are often *more* ruthless with one another than with a male counterpart. According to pretty much all psychological research, women are often harder on each other than men are on each other.

For example, research shows that women are less likely to be friends with women who are "sexually promiscuous," compared to men, who are more likely to be friends with other men who are sexually promiscuous.[1] Women are definitely more sensitive to social exclusion than men, and when they feel threatened by the thought of being left out, their first response may be to socially exclude another woman. A study examining aggressive attitudes and behavior of fourth- and fifth-grade boys and girls found that girls were significantly more victimized from a relational standpoint, while boys were significantly more victimized from a physical standpoint.[2] A mother's influence also plays a significant role: "Women who are mean-spirited about other women were often raised by a mother who probably didn't like herself and didn't feel warmly toward women, in general, either."[3] Finally, and most importantly, anxiety is a key factor: "The majority of female criticism actually stems from feeling inadequate in an area of life they value highly."[4] So, for example, an insecure woman might judge a secure woman to compensate for her anxiety around her own self-image.

Based on this research, I realized that this girl-on-girl aggression is rooted in the patriarchal system. Women seeing other women as sluts, versus men not thinking of sexually promiscuous men in a negative light, is clearly a response to what's "acceptable in society today" (that is, a patriarchal society)—otherwise it would be equal judgment on both sides. The same goes for the way women judge other women's appearance. It's all wrapped in current societal standards.

You might be thinking, *Yeah, but I know some women who do this and have very cool moms. Why would those kind of women be inclined to perpetuate girl-on-girl aggression?*

I was curious too, so I did some research, and the puzzle pieces started coming together.

ONE HYPOTHESIS: NEOLITHIC ERA PLAYED A ROLE IN GIRL-ON-GIRL CRIME

Going back historically into where this girl-on-girl hate might have come from, some would argue that many of these relational challenges among women (and between women and men) date back to the Neolithic Era (from about 10,200 B.C.E. to between 4,500 and 2,000 B.C.E.), when land started to get divided and "ownership" of land was created.[5] Splitting up land inadvertently created a scarcity mind-set because no longer was ALL land available to forage from. Since men are physically stronger than women, men took ownership of the land and made the women take their names.

Men then would say: "This is MY land, where I grow MY crops and feed MY herd and where MY woman must be a virgin so I know who MY offspring is so I can know who will own MY land and herd when I die. I have to protect my land because there is only enough to provide for MY family."

This scarcity mind-set was then passed on to women, who said: "Some people have larger portions than others, and I need to make sure I have food for MY children who have taken MY husband's name and that we are safe on the land and with the herd that MY husband now owns."

This potentially created competition among women to choose the men who had the most land (aka, they were the most secure).

I'm painting with super broad strokes here because everything is always way more complicated, but it's important to understand the big-picture concept. Prior to the Neolithic Era, women and men in the Paleolithic Era foraged for just what they needed, used the land as a group, and shared food and resources in community. There was no "ownership" of anything until land division became a thing in the Neolithic Era and everything changed. The "scarcity mind-set" became the breeding ground for much of human suffering thereafter and informed the way future businesses and world governments would operate. Women got stuck in this system and were then indoctrinated by it as well.

ANOTHER HYPOTHESIS: IS IT PRIMAL TOO?

Going back even further, many would argue from a purely animalistic point of view that girl-on-girl aggression is based on the primal instincts of females (versus males). Females generally choose one mate to procreate with, versus males, who want to spread their seed. Therefore today's current society might judge women differently than men because we take this natural instinct and turn it into a moral standard. (Women are negatively regarded if they hook up with a lot of men, while men are positively regarded if they hook up with a lot of women.)

AWARENESS IS KEY

Hopefully the more we understand where some of this girl-on-girl hate might have come from, the more we might choose to do things differently. It's on us to be aware of our own biases, to actively catch ourselves when we are judging or "hating on" other women. We need to recognize the history of where our judgments come from and question whether they should be relevant to us today or not. If they're not (and they're not), we need to throw those preconceived notions away. The more we catch ourselves in Neolithic thoughts and actions, the more unraveled by the patriarchal system we will be—and the happier we will be.

THE EXTERNAL VERSUS THE INTERNAL

When we are "hating on" someone externally, this often reflects where we are internally. It sounds obvious, but it's often hard to see this in the moment, when the claws are out and shit talkin' and chirping begin.

The **internal emotional spectrum** can be defined as the spectrum of emotions we feel at any given moment. It can range from happy, inspired, fulfilled, or secure to angry, hurt, sad, insecure, anxious, or jealous, depending on what we are experiencing throughout the day.

Moment by moment, different experiences trigger different emotions within us. We all teeter back and forth on the internal emotional spectrum throughout the day, and we must recognize that.

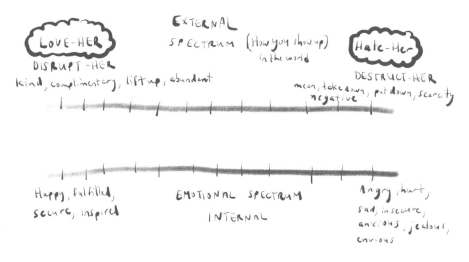

NOW LET'S TALK ABOUT THE "LOVE-HER TO HATE-HER" SPECTRUM.

A **Love-Her** is a generous woman who is kind and complimentary. She has an abundance mind-set and a generative spirit. She is a consummate champion of the women around her.

A **Hate-Her** acts out in a destructive manner and externally puts down or takes down other women to feel better about herself. She often acts in a mean-spirited, negative way. She has a scarcity mind-set and generally talks a lot of shit (in person or online as a troll).

Sometimes when we're feeling angry, hurt, insecure, anxious, jealous, or envious *internally*, we tend to be a Hate-Her *externally*—we act cruelly and negatively and attempt to take others down. When we're feeling happy, fulfilled, and secure internally, we become a Love-Her externally—we act kind, give compliments, and are generous.

The goal is to *be aware* of where we are in our *own* internal emotional spectrum and CATCH OURSELVES before we pass judgment and act out, which manifests externally as being a Hate-Her.

PEOPLE DON'T START OUT AS HATE-HERS

When we are born, we all start out as Love-Hers. We are bright-eyed and innocent and the world is magical and happy. Throughout our lives we get societal opinions piled on us, and judgments we feel others are placing on us and judgments we are placing on ourselves show up as the behavior of a Hate-Her, a mean girl, someone who wants to hurt someone else to mask her own pain.

So when I talk about Hate-Hers in this chapter, I really am talking about women ACTING OUT as Hate-Hers. They are NOT Hate-Hers inherently. There is a clear distinction here. Being a Hate-Her is a behavior that can be remedied; we can go back to being a Love-Her by simply understanding where the internal pain comes from and tackling it like the badass Disrupt-Hers that we are.

I'M NOT GIVING A FREE PASS TO HATE-HERS

Now, to be clear, this isn't meant to let anyone who acts out as a Hate-Her just slide. Sometimes a Hate-Her is aware that she is feeling bad, insecure, angry, down in the dumps, and vengeful, and she wants to make others around her feel as bad as she feels. And she knows that she might get away with it because people might "feel sorry for her" and the "pity party" might help her take advantage of the system even more:

"Aww, she doesn't know any better."

"She comes from a broken family."

"Look at the friends she hangs out with. Poor thing."

"She is hurting herself in the end anyway."

Some people mask their Hate-Her feelings as "VICTIMHOOD" to take advantage of the system. (The Drama Triangle below will help explain this further.)

People do spend a disproportionate amount of time trying to understand those who act out as Hate-Hers—actively listening to them, understanding that they sometimes come from dysfunctional families—when the same time and energy could be spent on people who are doing their best and who *didn't hurt anyone*. The good ones sometimes are *not* getting the support or the leg up that Hate-Hers are getting, even if their family circumstances are the same.

Often the kid in the family who is misbehaving gets the most attention. Or in class the good kids are often overlooked. At work too the ones who get the most attention are the most troublesome ones.

Often the people who are doing it right are ignored, overlooked, and taken for granted, because they are not causing problems. So whether we are a parent, a leader, or a friend, we need to consciously make sure we are noticing the people in our lives who have an absence of these negative behaviors. Hate-Hers are choosing on some level to act out, even if they sometimes don't know any better. Also, the time spent trying to figure out how to get Hate-Hers back to being Love-Hers is part of the psychological drama and disproportionate negative impact that Hate-Hers have.

Since the "fight-or-flight" part of our brain (our amygdala) chooses to prioritize the negative first, we focus more on Hate-Hers than on Love-Hers.

And rewarded behavior gets repeated. So if we are giving too much of our time and attention to Hate-Hers, they'll just keep acting out. The more we focus our time and attention on the Love-Hers, the more likely the Hate-Hers will have to rejigger themselves to get back to their original loving state (because we all began as Love-Hers).

WE MUST RECOGNIZE THAT *TIME* IS THE MOST NONRENEWABLE RESOURCE WE HAVE, SO WE MUST FOCUS OUR TIME AND ATTENTION ON THINGS THAT SERVE OUR HIGHEST SELVES (LOVE-HERS), NOT CATER TO THE LOWEST COMMON DENOMINATOR (HATE-HERS).

Let's ask ourselves, *Who are we going to choose to reward with our attention and time?*

THE DRAMA TRIANGLE: A NEGATIVE REINFORCEMENT LOOP

Now that we understand where negative girl-on-girl feelings may come from and how they can be manipulated, we might be able to better understand the Drama Triangle.

Stephen Karpman, M.D., came up with the concept of the Drama Triangle in 1968. I consulted Wikipedia to get to the bottom of it. This is how they break it down:

- **THE VICTIM.** The victim's stance is "Poor me!" The victim feels "victimized, oppressed, helpless, hopeless, powerless, ashamed, and seems unable to make decisions, solve problems, take pleasure in life, or achieve insight." When a Hate-Her is playing this role, she is not proactively solving her problems; she is waiting for others to solve them for her. (Note that this is the victim *mentality* we are going after, not actual people who have been *real victims* of unfortunate or worse incidents.)

- **THE PERSECUTOR.** Also known as the villain. The persecutor insists, "It's all your fault." The persecutor is "controlling, blaming, critical, oppressive, angry, authoritative, rigid, and superior." When a Hate-Her is in this role, she is blaming others and choosing to tear another down instead of productively helping people and holding them to being their highest selves.

- **THE RESCUER.** The rescuer's line is "Let me help you." A classic enabler, the rescuer feels "guilty if he/she doesn't go to the rescue. This rescue role is also very pivotal because their actual primary interest is really an avoidance of their own problems disguised as concern for the victim's needs." When a Hate-Her plays this role, she is choosing to help with the PITY PARTY, enabling the victim to further feel helpless, instead of productively holding space for the victim and helping resolve the issue positively. Internet trolls can often be found in this role— they sometimes present themselves as "social justice warriors" and unproductively troll people, hiding behind the walls of the Internet, to get some of their own personal angst out.

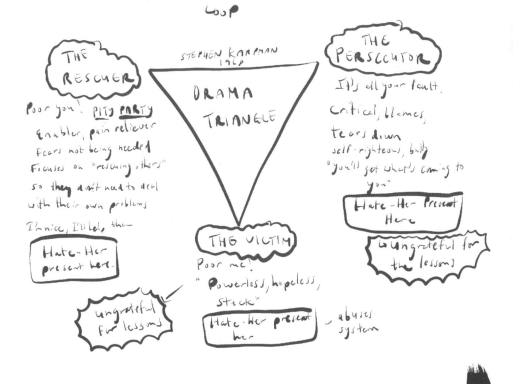

According to Wikipedia, Karpman states that "Initially, a drama triangle comes about when a person takes on the role of a victim or persecutor. This person then feels the need to bring in other people into the conflict. As often happens, a rescuer is encouraged to enter the situation. These enlisted players take on roles of their own that are not static, and therefore various scenarios can occur. For example, the victim might turn on the rescuer, the rescuer then switches to persecuting."

This clearly showcases a negative reinforcement loop where each participant gets their needs met in a justified way, "without having to acknowledge the broader dysfunction or harm done in the situation as a whole" (the perfect breeding ground for a Hate-Her mind-set). "As such, each participant is acting upon their own selfish needs, rather than acting in a genuinely responsible or altruistic manner." There is negativity and blame in every aspect of the Drama Triangle instead of productive opportunities for growth.

Let's go back to the beginning of this chapter, where, to mask her own hurt, Jen accused Lisa of something that Lisa didn't do. Here, Jen pretended to be the victim but was in fact the persecutor. Rather than taking ownership of being a challenging roommate and productively being better the next time around, Jen chose to accuse Lisa of wrongdoing and enlisted her friends (the pity party) to play rescuer. No part of this triangle has any integrity; it is all based in the Hate-Her mind-set.

THE DISRUPT-HER TRIANGLE: A POSITIVE REINFORCEMENT LOOP

Rather than focusing on the negative reinforcement loop, Disrupt-Hers focus on a positive reinforcement loop, which I call the Disrupt-Her Triangle, consisting of the Disrupt-Her, the Darer, and the Mentor. The Love-Her is present in each corner of the Disrupt-Her Triangle.

- **THE DISRUPT-HER.** The Disrupt-Her chooses to NEVER be the victim, no matter the circumstance, and chooses to move forward productively. She understands that the human experience isn't perfect for anyone, that we all go through so many ups and downs in life, and that the only way to get past negative experiences is to learn from them and productively move forward with gratitude for the expanded emotional capacity. She sees every experience as an opportunity to learn and gain inner strength. She consistently takes positive, tangible steps to resolve problems. (The Disrupt-Her replaces the victim—"Poor me!"—in the Drama Triangle.)

- **THE DARER.** The Darer doesn't blame others or point fingers; instead, she productively dares the Disrupt-Her to be great the next time around; she challenges her to grow and sets clear boundaries to play and work in next time. (The Darer replaces the persecutor—"It's all your fault!"—in the Drama Triangle.)

- **THE MENTOR.** The Mentor doesn't hop on any negative bandwagon or enable the Disrupt-Her to spiral downward. She offers space for the Disrupt-Her to purge her thoughts and feelings and helps organize them. She holds the Disrupt-Her accountable for her actions and sees the Disrupt-Her as her highest self. (The Mentor replaces the rescuer—"I'll save you!" in the Drama Triangle.)

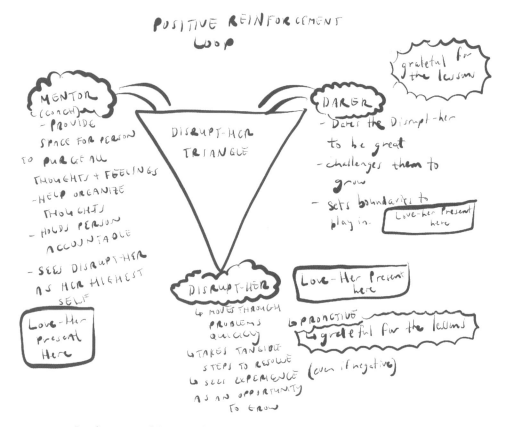

POSITIVE REINFORCEMENT LOOP

grateful for the lesson

MENTOR (COACH)
- PROVIDE SPACE FOR PERSON TO PURGE ALL THOUGHTS + FEELINGS
- HELP ORGANIZE THOUGHTS
- HOLDS PERSON ACCOUNTABLE
- SEES DISRUPT-HER AS HER HIGHEST SELF

Love-Her present Here

DISRUPT-HER TRIANGLE

DARER
- Dares the Disrupt-her to be great
- challenges them to grow
- sets boundaries to play in

Love-Her Present here

DISRUPT-HER
↳ MOVES THROUGH PROBLEMS QUICKLY
↳ PROACTIVE
↳ grateful for the lessons (even if negative)
↳ TAKES TANGIBLE STEPS TO RESOLVE
↳ SEES EXPERIENCE AS AN OPPORTUNITY TO GROW

Love-Her Present here

In the case of Lisa and Jen, here's the way their situation could have played out as a positive reinforcement loop (Disrupt-Her Triangle) instead of a negative reinforcement loop (Drama Triangle):

Once Lisa told Jen that she was moving out, Jen (Disrupt-Her) would have been grateful for the lessons learned in this experience, would take tangible steps to resolve and move through the problems quickly for the next go-round, and would see the experience of Lisa moving out as an opportunity to grow as a human. Lisa (Darer) would have then been able to dare Jen to be great the next time around and positively challenge her to grow. And Jen would have enlisted her friends (Mentors) to share what happened and hold her accountable to be great with the next roommate. Every part of this triangle has integrity and is based in the Love-Her mind-set.

We must catch ourselves when we are in a negative reinforcement loop that feels like we can justify what we're doing and why we're doing it, and then transmute it into a positive reinforcement loop—going from Hate-Her to Love-Her.

As soon as we get to the bottom of our own internal emotional state and understand our underlying feelings, we'll be able to handle the external treatment of others with so much more love, understanding, and most importantly, gratitude.

As Martin Luther King, Jr., said so beautifully, "Darkness cannot drive out darkness; only light can do that. Hate cannot drive out hate; only love can do that."

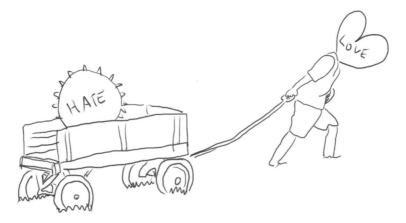

INTEGRITY

Integrity plays an integral role in the process of becoming a Disrupt-Her, and if we don't understand what it truly means, we'll never *fully* embody the Disrupt-Her.

Lauren, my life coach (from the Handel Group) and my Mentor in my Disrupt-Her Triangle, taught me that being "in integrity" means that **everything we are thinking, feeling, and saying has to match up.**

Here are a couple of examples of NOT being in integrity:

"Hi, Mary! You look amazing! Did you get a haircut? I love it!" (saying out loud)

Your haircut makes your face look fat. (thinking)

Why didn't you call me when you said you would? I'm hurt. (feeling)
Or:

"Hi, Sandy! How are you?" (saying out loud)

Bitch. (thinking)

I can't believe you slept with my ex—even though I gave you permission to date him after we broke up, you should have known better. (feeling)

Far too often, we are not in integrity at all with what we're thinking, feeling, and saying, and we end up wasting our time talking shit about the other person to someone else, rather than actually facing them ourselves. A Disrupt-Her is not afraid to have tough conversations directly with the person she is having an issue with.

Here is how you would be "in integrity" in the above two situations:

"Hey Mary, I've noticed this is the third time you said you'd call me and didn't. That makes me feel like you don't respect our friendship. Is there anything that's going on that I can help you with, or is there something you want to talk about?" (saying out loud)

Why didn't you call me when you said you would? I want to understand. (thinking)

Why didn't you call me when you said you would? I'm hurt. (feeling)

And:

"Hey Sandy, I really appreciate you asking me first if you could date my ex, and I know I said it was totally fine, but after thinking about it, it actually does bother me. I know I can't stop you from pursuing it; I'd just rather not see it right now. I'm sure in time it'll get easier, and I'll let you know when that is. Can we agree to that, do you think?" (saying out loud)

I'm not happy that you're dating my ex, and I need time to heal. (thinking)

I'm sad that you're dating my ex, even though I told you it was okay to date him after we broke up. My heart (and ego) is still healing. (feeling)

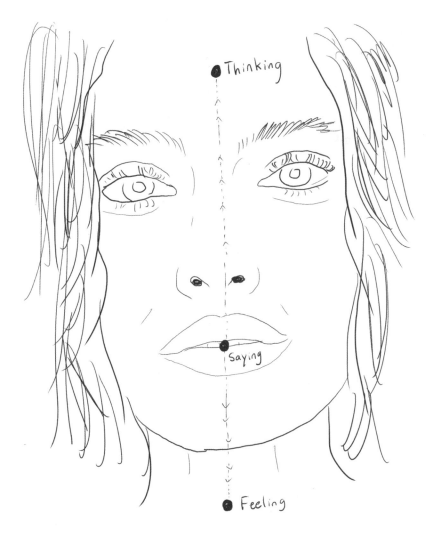

See what happens when you are in alignment in your head, heart, and voice? It feels SO much better and is so much less to manage, right?

So any time you find yourself NOT in alignment with the three, catch yourself and write down what you're thinking, feeling, and saying. You'll see where the discrepancy is and have the courage to face the people you have issues with. You'll realize how often you aren't in alignment. The more you catch yourself, the faster you'll recognize the pattern you have for not being honest with yourself and the people around you. And the more you catch yourself, the less negative you'll feel (your internal spectrum of emotion) and the less likely you will be to act out as a Hate-Her.

SPEAK IT KINDLY

When you do speak your truth, do it kindly, lovingly, and with curiosity, like you would with an innocent child, never raising your voice or getting upset. I have made the mistake in the past of losing my cool with people I was frustrated with, and it didn't serve either of us. Even if I was "in integrity" with what I was thinking, feeling, and saying, I sometimes spoke unkindly, which often didn't make the person receive what I said in the way I wanted them to. All they were thinking about was *how* I had spoken, and they went on the defensive right away and didn't hear my point at all. So the WAY we say things, even when we are in integrity, is critical in opening up hearts and minds. A message is only as good as its ability to be received.

PUTTING IT ALL TOGETHER

To be a Disrupt-Her, you must (1) get back to your childlike state of curiosity, playfulness, and awe; (2) practice addition by subtraction in all facets of your life; (3) figure out what your LIT path is as opposed to a traditional "career path"; (4) start investing your money wisely; (5) become a Warrior Gatekeeper of your mind by actively catching what comes to your mental gate (and then practicing pattern interruption if you do accidentally let in a negative thought and start spiraling out of control); (6) iterate and get better every day in all the things you're doing instead of focusing on being perfect; and (7) catch yourself when you're being a Hate-Her by understanding where you are in your life personally and where you are not in integrity. Easy, right? ;-)

DISRUPTION #7

EXERCISES

1. To really understand where you're at when it comes to dealing with Love-Hers and Hate-Hers, ask yourself:

   - How much time did I spend today thinking and talking about the negative person(s) in my life?

   - How much time did I spend thinking and talking about people who are in integrity, who are supportive of me, and who are adding value and showing up in the world in good ways?

2. Every time you start thinking about a person who is acting out as a Hate-Her, get curious about where the bad behavior comes from. Practice being the Warrior Gatekeeper of your mind and catching negative thoughts about that person before they spiral out of control.

3. When you face women who are acting out as Hate-Hers at work or in your personal life, do not enable them and do not blame them. Spend some time helping them to understand their

internal spectrum of emotion and how that might affect their external demeanor, but otherwise choose to focus your time and attention on Love-Hers—those who choose to be in a positive reinforcement loop. Release the Hate-Hers as soon as you see that they are not interested in transmuting their Drama Triangle to a Disrupt-Her Triangle.

4. Understand who and what you're not in integrity with. Every time you catch yourself thinking, feeling, saying things that don't align, write it down.

5. When another woman is creating value in the world, cheer her on and offer your help. If you feel a pang of jealousy or envy in your own internal spectrum of emotion, catch yourself and choose to enter a positive reinforcement loop instead. Being a Love-Her will always serve your highest self and you will be proud that you have chosen this path—and it will help you get to your most actualized self faster.

RB ACCOUNTABILIBUDDY
ACTION #7!

**ACTING OUT AS A "HATE-HER" IS NEVER
SOMETHING THAT YOU FEEL GOOD ABOUT.**

IN ANY MOMENT THAT YOU'RE FEELING LIKE
A HATE-HER AND WANT TO TAKE SOMEONE DOWN
TO GIVE YOU THAT HA! I MADE YOU FEEL AS SHITTY
AS I DO! FEELING, KNOW THAT IT ALWAYS ENDS UP IN REGRET
AND DEEPER SELF-LOATHING. (IT'S KINDA LIKE EATING FAST FOOD—
IT FEELS GOOD GOING DOWN AFTER A DRUNKEN NIGHT,
BUT THE NEXT DAY YOU WANT TO CRAWL INTO A HOLE.)

RATHER THAN TAKING SOMEONE DOWN WITH YOU
AS YOU ARE EXPERIENCING THE NEGATIVE SIDE OF YOUR
INTERNAL SPECTRUM OF EMOTION, CHECK IN WITH
YOUR ACCOUNTABILIBUDDY INSTEAD:

WHENEVER YOU FEEL YOURSELF WANTING TO ACT OUT AS
A **HATE-HER**, RB IS ASKING YOU TO TAKE
HER OFF YOUR WRIST, TWIST HER AROUND YOUR LEFT THUMB
AND THEN TAKE 60 SECONDS TO TEXT A FRIEND THE FOLLOWING:

"I'M PLAYING A FUN GAME.
ONE THING I LIKE ABOUT YOU IS_____."

BY POINTING OUT THE GOOD IN OTHERS,
WE ARE REMINDED OF THE GOOD IN OURSELVES.

OR, IF YOU WANT TO PRACTICE BEING IN INTEGRITY,
WHEN YOU CATCH YOURSELF NOT BEING IN INTEGRITY ABOUT
SOMEONE WHO IS ON YOUR MIND, TEXT THEM THIS:
"HEY_____! WOULD LOVE TO GET TEA [OR FACETIME IF NOT IN SAME CITY]
AND CATCH UP AND SHARE SOME THOUGHTS
I AM HAVING. LET ME KNOW IF YOU'RE AROUND THIS WEEK!"

THEN FIND TIME TO CONNECT WITH THEM AND KINDLY SHARE
WHAT YOU'RE FEELING WITH ALL THE LOVE IN YOUR HEART.
THE MORE INTEGRITY YOU HAVE, THE MORE LIKELY
SHE IS TO ACT LIKE A **LOVE-HER** TOWARD YOU IN RETURN.

THIS NEXT CHAPTER
IS LITERALLY WRITTEN
BACKWARD.
THE FIRST PAGE OF
THIS CHAPTER WILL ACTUALLY
BE ON THE LAST PAGE
OF THIS CHAPTER,
AND YOU WILL HAVE TO
READ IT FROM THE
RIGHT SIDE TO THE LEFT.
BECAUSE WHY NOT?
THAT'S THE POINT.

NOW FLIP TO THE LAST PAGE
OF THIS CHAPTER TO READ IT.

RB ACCOUNTABILIBUDDY
ACTION #8!

**DREAMING UP YOUR POSITIVE,
DISRUPTIVE CONTRIBUTION CAN BE SO FUN!**

TAKING REAL, TANGIBLE ACTION CAN
SEEM SCARY IN THE BEGINNING.
THE ONLY WAY TO GET GOOD AT IT IS TO PRACTICE,
PRACTICE, PRACTICE! THIS IS OFFICIALLY THE
TIME FOR YOU TO FIGURE OUT WHAT,
WHERE, AND HOW YOU WANT TO BE A
DISRUPT-HER IN THIS WORLD, WHILE YOU ARE HERE
AND ALIVE FOR A SHORT AMOUNT OF TIME.

WHENEVER YOU START THINKING ABOUT
WHAT YOUR DISRUPTIVE CONTRIBUTION IS,
RB IS ASKING YOU TO FLIP HER OVER
SO YOU CAN EXPOSE HER UNDERBELLY AND HEART,
WHICH WILL GIVE YOU PERMISSION TO
EXPOSE YOUR UNDERBELLY AND HEART,
TAKE A LOOK DEEP INSIDE, AND ASK YOURSELF
WHAT YOU WANT TO DISRUPT IN THE WORLD.

BY **COMMITTING** TO MAKE A
**POSITIVE, DISRUPTIVE
CONTRIBUTION** TO THE WORLD
(NOW, NOT LATER!), WE WILL HOPEFULLY ALL
REMEMBER THAT WE ARE STEWARDS OF
THIS PLANET   AND OF

THE PEOPLE THAT FOLLOW US,
AND WE HAVE MAGICAL SUPERPOWERS
TO TRULY
MAKE A DIFFERENCE.

DISRUPTION #8

EXERCISES

1. Write down three things right now in your world that you might question. It could be anything, like "Why do we read from left to right?" This is to practice putting your mind in a disruptive state.

2. Start looking around your world for the things that make you feel upset or sad or confused, and use those feelings as fuel to get really curious and passionate about figuring out how to improve them.

3. Ask yourself, *What's stopping me from boldly going after what gets me fired up now?*

4. Think about a problem you'd like to tackle. First, find an organization or business that is working on disrupting the thing you're interested in and see how you can support them. It's a great way to get started and begin flexing your mental muscle in thinking outside the box.

PUTTING IT ALL TOGETHER

To be a Disrupt-Her, you must (1) get back to your childlike state of curiosity, playfulness, and awe; (2) practice addition by subtraction in all facets of your life; (3) figure out what your LIT path is as opposed to a traditional "career path"; (4) start investing your money wisely; (5) become a Warrior Gatekeeper of your mind by actively catching what comes to your mental gate (and then practicing pattern interruption if you do accidentally let in a negative thought and start spiraling out of control); (6) iterate and get better every day in all the things you're doing, instead of focusing on being perfect; (7) catch yourself when you're being a Hate-Her by understanding where you are in your life personally and where you are not in integrity; and (8) embody your Disrupt-Her, question the status quo, and know that YOU have the ability to make a difference if you just get curious and passionate about something that doesn't make sense in the world. It's time to figure out what your unique, positive, disruptive contribution will be, whether big or small!

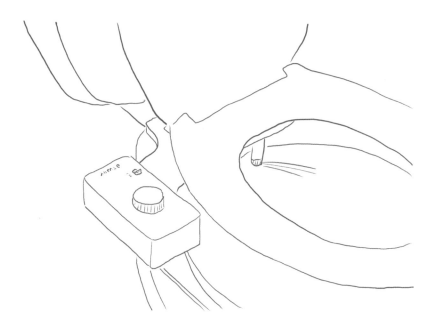

A great perk about disrupting the status quo is that these challenges attract other interested, curious, self-starting people! I have a fabulous team of self-motivated people who are equally as passionate about breaking this age-old poop taboo!

Are you getting excited about your area of disruption? What can you get excited about and put your energy toward that disrupts the status quo? You should have those excited butterflies and renewed feelings of "I GOT THIS" bubbling inside your belly, especially since you now have the tools to truly disrupt the current way of thinking.

We have more access to information today than ever before (thank you, Google, YouTube, and the Internet in general), so now it's time to look at all the information available, see where things don't make sense anymore, and take the initiative to PRESS GO!

wait till it's dark outside, walk several miles with other women for protection, and then relieve themselves. This is a DAILY struggle for girls and women in many parts of the world, which I cannot imagine having to endure.

I found a great organization called Samagra that brings clean latrines to communities that desperately need them. And rather than just building a latrine and leaving the people to fend for themselves right off the bat (like many NGOs do), Samagra teaches the community how to use the latrines and how to keep them clean. They spend six months working with the community (through an incentive program) to maintain it, and then once the community starts seeing the vast improvements in the health of their families and in their living conditions, they understand its benefit and begin to care for it properly. Once it's a well-running facility, Samagra then moves on to support another community.

This opportunity to disrupt the status quo, not only in America but globally, became even more exciting to me. I got really curious about this space and found a true passion for wanting to improve it.

And so TUSHY was officially born. We created a simple, modern, beautiful, affordable, best-in-class bidet attachment (it looks like an iPhone attached to your toilet) that clips onto any ordinary American toilet and turns it into a bidet without any plumbing or electrical required (none of those French contraptions next to the toilet that take up space and require plumbing, etc.) and sets up in 10 minutes flat. We are helping save millions of trees and relieving people of health problems, and we're bringing light to the global sanitation crisis at the same time. We have formed a partnership with Samagra, and to date we have helped well over 10,000 families in India gain access to clean latrines. I cannot wait for that number to be in the millions! We all live on the same spaceship called Earth, and the fact that you and I won the lottery of life by being born where we have is an important thing to recognize. I believe it's our duty to get curious and passionate about disrupting problems locally and globally for people who are right here on the same planet as we are.

thinking that we "need" this consumable (the industry's preferred term for "disposable") product. Big companies want us to start "depending" on disposables so we will keep buying the products over and over again, which is great for big business but terrible for our health, the environment, and our wallets.

And, really? How on earth did we fall for these big companies telling us that DRY PAPER will *actually clean* our butts? Imagine if someone told you to jump in the shower and instead of using water to get yourself clean, use dry paper instead. Imagine if someone told you to wash your dirty dishes with dry paper, without any water. You'd laugh, right?

So what's the solution? Simple: a bidet.

The problem is that bidets have been stigmatized in the United States for decades for a number of reasons, and we know that BIG toilet paper companies want to keep it that way. They don't care that the equivalent of Central Park is getting chopped down every single day for American consumption of toilet paper. Who knows, they might even be in cahoots with BIG pharmaceutical companies who are making billions on UTI medication and hemorrhoid creams (since these problems are exacerbated by toilet paper). Hmmm, right?

I got really excited about the opportunity to rebrand another taboo category and reintroduce a bidet to the American market in a cool, relevant way.

At the same time, I also discovered the massive global sanitation crisis that is affecting billions of people. Over a billion people practice open defecation (pooping out in the open), which can have massive consequences, contaminating communities' water systems and causing people to get sick, not to mention that the living conditions are atrocious. (Can you imagine living in a place where the sight and smell of poop is everywhere you walk? I can't.) I also found out that girls and women are WAY more at risk for getting raped when there is nowhere safe for them to relieve themselves, as they can be vulnerable when in a position with their skirts down. So even today, millions of girls have to hold in their pee and their poop all day long (which is also bad for their health),

We created a business model called "Buy One, Fund One" where we gave money to a local Ugandan for-profit company (that we selected) that manufactured reusable menstrual pads. With the money that we provided them, they were able to offset the cost of the menstrual pads and then sell them affordably to local Ugandan women.

It became an exciting challenge for me personally to change culture—to disrupt the way people had viewed something for hundreds of years.

BREAKING THE POOP TABOO GLOBALLY

I have recently moved on from breaking the period taboo and have since gotten curious and incredibly passionate about solving problems around the other hole "down there": the butthole.

I realized that the nether regions have had little innovation because it's a space that people feel very uncomfortable talking about. This is so strange to me, because it's the region of the body that creates the most pleasure, it creates life, and it removes the things that the body doesn't need. And yet we neglect it so much (we almost run away from it) and haven't innovated in this category in close to a hundred years, especially in the butt department.

The more I got curious about it and the more research I did, the more passionate I became and the more I wanted to disrupt the current American thinking in this area too.

I discovered that 15 million trees get cut down every year to make toilet paper. I found out that toilet paper helps cause and/ or exacerbate 30 million cases of urinary tract infections, hemorrhoids, and yeast infections (and dingleberries). Wet wipes are even worse for the environment (the plastic microfibers don't biodegrade and end up polluting oceans and poisoning fish), and these wipes also cause anal fissures and anal itching because of the chemicals that strip the natural oils from our behinds. All of it costs a lot of money, and big companies have spent billions of dollars marketing these products and indoctrinating our culture into

DISRUPTIVE CHALLENGE ACCEPTED

"Do you have period-stained underwear in the back of your drawer too?" I asked a random woman.

"Excuse me?"

"I'm just asking a simple question."

"Um, that doesn't seem very appropriate to ask." (*Disgusted woman exits stage left.*)

When I realized that periods were uncomfortable to talk about, even for women, I discovered the shame that our current masculine society places on women around the most natural occurrence ever. Every woman bears the burden to bleed every single month in order to perpetuate the human species (which includes men, by the way), and yet this blood is considered shameful? And women are ridiculed all over the world for *this*? Girls are even held back in school because they don't have access to menstrual products, so they stay home during that week and get too far behind to keep up and many often quit school? What!?

NO WAY. COME ON. REALLY?! was my internal dialogue.

I grew incredibly curious and passionate about this as I researched and learned about this unfair taboo bestowed upon women.

After my twin sister and I came up with the period-proof underwear idea at our family barbecue, we brought in a third co-founder, Antonia, to create the product with us. Our goal was improving the way girls and women experience their periods through an innovative new underwear that didn't leak or stain, that absorbed blood, that wicked away the moisture (and was a beautiful, sexy pair to boot!), at the same time helping girls and women in the developing world gain access to basic menstrual products. And ultimately we wanted to disrupt this age-old taboo that was making women feel insecure instead of empowered.

We spent three and a half years developing the underwear technology, and we created an initial giveback partnership with an organization in Uganda that manufactured menstrual pads affordably.

MY PATH TO BECOMING A DISRUPT-HER

I didn't know that I could *really* disrupt anything in the business world until I started questioning why things were done a certain way myself and realized that I could *actually* do something about it.

When I graduated from college, I got a job in investment banking. I didn't want the job, but at the time it was the most sought-after job and the one that paid the most, and since I had real student loans to pay off and wanted to move to New York City with a prestigious job, I pushed away the thoughts of *NOOOOO* to make it happen. My subway stop every morning to go to my investment banking job was 2 World Trade Center, and I was supposed to be there exactly when the first plane hit on September 11, 2001.

But somehow I slept through my alarm clock and missed the whole thing. This was the first and only time in my life that I slept through my alarm clock. (I'm a very light sleeper and usually wake up at any tiny sound, but on that day I slept through it all.) Seven hundred people in my girlfriend's office died, and two people in my office died. This experience set me on a maniacal journey to live life fully lit up and to solve as many problems that crossed my path as I could. In my first book, *Do Cool Sh*t*, I wrote about having tummy aches, which led me to discover the massive processed food industry, which then led me to start my first business, WILD (EatDrinkWild.com), a gluten-free, farm-to-table pizza concept (which still exists to this day). I realized there were over a billion obese people on the planet in addition to a billion hungry people on the planet, and I wanted to do something about that. Offering healthy comfort food to the American world was a good place to start.

After a few years of growing the restaurant, I brought in a more appropriate (and wonderful and honest) restaurant operator, Walid (who is WAYYY more experienced than I am), to run the restaurant business, which then freed up my time to focus on my next disruptions: breaking the period and poop taboos.

Malala is a soft-spoken Pakistani teenager who was a Disrupt-Her long before the world knew her name. She didn't have an extroverted nature or what you might have seen in a "classic leader," but what she did have was passion, relentless conviction, and true integrity, which is all it took to turn her into a leader who challenged the world. She wasn't negative; she didn't yell angrily; she inspired people around her passionately and positively.

Can we each find a problem—small or big—or an old, tired stigma in our communities or in the world that we could get curious and passionate about? And can we find the challenge exciting enough to disrupt the status quo?

WINNING THE LOTTERY OF LIFE

In my own self-reflection, I very much understand that in so many ways, I won the lottery of life. On this one tiny planet, I could have been born in a mud hut or shanty shack in a developing part of the world where clean drinking water is five miles away, food is scarce, health care unfeasible, and girls have little to no access to things like education, menstrual products, or toilets. I could have been born and sold as a sex slave or for slave labor. I could have been born in a refugee camp without any opportunities. I understand that this reality exists for millions of people globally.

And instead, on this same tiny planet, I was born to two loving parents in war-free Canada, where clean drinking water, healthy food, and menstrual products are easily accessible, and where girls and women have basic human rights.

My parents taught me to never take any of this for granted, and that if we saw something in the world that needed fixing, we absolutely could do something about it.

Now it's your turn. It's your turn to look in the mirror and see a Disrupt-Her reflected back, someone who is helping improve the world, breaking old barriers that need breaking, and eliminating societal stigmas that need to be eliminated.

MALALA

A clear example of someone making a seemingly small contribution and it having compounding effects is wonder-girl Malala Yousafzai. When she was only 15 years old, Malala stood up to the Taliban in Pakistan by speaking out as an advocate for girls' education. The Taliban wanted to maintain control of Pakistani women, and they knew education would strengthen the women, so they did everything they could to keep girls and women from learning. They issued a death threat against Malala and eventually shot her in the face while she was coming home from school. Really? They were *that* scared of what educated girls could do that they had to shoot a teenager in the face? Makes us women feel pretty damn badass in a twisted way, doesn't it? Malala miraculously survived, and instead of retreating or playing the victim, she powerfully fought back, and her story brought so much light to the importance of girls' education and the positive impact it has in the world. Had Malala not challenged the status quo, girls and women would be so much farther behind.

"BUT LIKE, WHO CARES? I READ HOW I READ. DO I REALLY NEED TO START QUESTIONING EVERYTHING IN MY LIFE NOW?"

The answer is YES—this is the whole point. And have fun with it!

The goal here is to make us all question everything in our lives and all our beliefs—things we just accept as "the way it is" or "the truth"—and ask ourselves if we can make our own contribution in rethinking those things.

Some of you might say: "Look, I get it and really want to be a Disrupt-Her too and question stuff, but (a) it sounds exhausting, and (b) I'm not really an extroverted, 'loud 'n' proud,' 'disruptive' type. I'm introverted, self-conscious in crowds, and have never been 'the leader' in a group. I'm the quiet one. Why would anyone follow what I have to say? So while I totally get what it takes to be a Disrupt-Her, I'm not sure you're describing ME."

Nowhere did I say you need to be "LOUD" and "EXTRO-VERTED" to be a Disrupt-Her, though some people have this mis-conception. Practicing the first seven disruptions in this book will certainly set you on a very clear path to becoming the strong, powerful Disrupt-Her that you want to be in your own life, as loud or as quiet as you want.

The key thing to understand in this chapter is that absolutely EVERYONE can make a significant contribution to the world and disrupt something that is not working in today's society. It all begins by taking small actions, first in your own life, for yourself, as described in the first seven disruptions in the book, and then in the world, which can have compounding ripple effects.

So it would make sense that this chapter is written backward, right?

(That was a rhetorical question—but maybe you're the rare soul that it already *does* make sense to!)

"OKAY, YOU GOT ME—WHY IS THIS CHAPTER WRITTEN BACKWARD?"

The better question to ask is, why is most text written from left to right and not from right to left? Have you ever asked yourself that?

It's been hypothesized that this is because "right-handed scribes would smudge their work if they wrote from right to left," and most humans (70–95 percent according to *Scientific American*) are right-handed.[1]

"SO WAIT, ARE YOU TELLING ME THAT WE'RE STILL READING THE WAY PEOPLE READ IN THE BABYLONIAN ERA?"

It certainly made sense to do this when everything was scribed in ink, but now that we have computers, shouldn't we question why we're still reading the same way we did thousands of years ago? Couldn't there be a more efficient way to read that we haven't thought about because we never questioned it before?

DISRUPTION #8

Don't think too big
(especially if you're a woman).

Always think BIG.
Everyone can be a Disrupt-Her.

Congratulations! You have made it past the halfway point of becoming the most disruptive, society-busting, light-filled, iterative-process-loving, self-assured, self-inquiring, Love-Her-ing, full-of-integrity, kind version of yourself. Phew! Now it's time to figure out what you plan on disrupting in the world, whether big or small.

In order to disrupt the status-quo mind-set, you must start practicing by questioning everything in your world.

DISRUPTION #9

Don't rock the boat.

DISRUPTION

Rock the boat and fight
the patriarchy authentically.

"Are you a feminist?" the reporter asked.

"Is that a trick question?" I was trying to size her up.

"What do you mean?" she responded, innocently.

"Well, do I believe in gender equality? Of course I do. A big part of my life's work is to invent products that improve women's lives. But do I relate to the term 'feminist' in its current context? I'm not so sure."

"Why not?" she sat up straighter and adjusted her phone to make sure it was still recording.

"Well, it's fraught with connotation and nuance, and I'm not sure I want to get into a war of 'how feminist I actually am.'"

"What kind of war?"

I had read up on this particular reporter before the interview and knew that she was hoping to "catch" me saying something controversial that would create a great clickbait headline to really get the "social justice warriors" going. I know that some reporters choose to write clickbait, takedown pieces no matter what the truth is and some reporters choose to write pieces with journalistic integrity. This particular reporter seemed to be the former.

"That I don't fit into the exact box of feminism that others deem to be the 'correct version'?"

"And what is the correct version of feminism?" The reporter was almost licking her lips, like an animal about to get a big, bloody feast.

DISRUPT-HER

"Well, it depends on the type of group that is scrutinizing me. Some might say I don't have all the feminist jargon down, so how could I be a 'real feminist'? Others might say I 'co-opted the term "feminism" as a marketing tactic' for my businesses. And to that, I start by saying, 'Well, isn't that awesome? Because the term "feminism" was the most societally hated word for so long—so it's great that at least it's a positive term that can be "used for marketing" now!' I follow that up with 'And no, I am not "using feminism for marketing"; my businesses are inherently feminist because they alleviate undue societal shame for women, and my products help all humans gain more confidence to level the playing field every day.' So yeah, it's hard sometimes to relate to the actual term and check every feminist subgroup's box of 'real feminism,' but am I wholeheartedly all about equal rights for all humans? Yes, I am."

I was speaking from my heart, and it didn't matter whether or not this reporter took things I said out of context to create a dramatic headline ("Female Founder of Feminist Company Doesn't Relate to the Term 'Feminism' Yet Uses Feminism for Marketing!"—there, I just gave it to you). I was actually so grateful for this "gotcha" exchange because it made me dream of what the world would look like if women (and good men) decided what metrics were important in society (like how kind, supportive, and uplifting we can be versus catering to our lowest selves, which is what we end up doing in the trap of the masculine system that promotes power and control). We are still a long way away from a truly equal (and feminine) mind-set in society, and I was glad to be reminded of the work we still have ahead of us.

(Sidebar: The reason that some media and social media cater to our "lowest selves" is that our amygdala, the fight-or-flight part of our brain, gets triggered first—so if headlines are negative, take-down-y, and gossipy, people will be more likely to click on them, compared to an uplifting, thoughtful, loving headline. The media is competing for our attention and will do whatever it needs to do to get our attention first in order to maintain happy advertisers. A pretty shitty incentive that doesn't promote integrity or authenticity, right? It's on us to catch ourselves before we click on the negative stuff that caters to our worst selves. These metrics "to keep the advertisers happy," with no regard for the damage that these negative headlines do to people, is another clear sign that the patriarchal system that promotes power, control, and domination is alive and well. We can control what gets served to us in social media based on what we click on, so can we please NOT click on the low-vibrational, inflamed stuff moving forward? The more we choose what we put our attention toward, the more the world can be a kinder, more loving place. The argument back would be: "Yes, but how do I know what's clickbait and what's real?" My response is: "Do one layer of research and you'll know." The media *will* adjust their headlines based on what *we* choose to focus our time and attention on.)

Let's rewind here and start from the beginning to understand where the patriarchal system came from, the growing feminist movement, and the way forward to get to true, loving gender equality among all humans.

The world is changed by your example,
not by your opinion.

PAULO COELHO

THE PATRIARCHY DECONSTRUCTED

In order for women, together with good men, to truly disrupt the patriarchal system, we need to understand where the patriarchy even came from.

TO RECOGNIZE THE GREAT MEN IN THE WORLD TODAY WHO TREAT WOMEN EQUALLY AND WITH RESPECT, I WANT TO MAKE A CLEAR DISTINCTION THAT WHEN I REFER TO A MAN CURRENTLY STUCK IN THE PATRIARCHY, I WILL REFER TO HIM AS A PM—PATRIARCHAL MAN.

As I described in Chapter 7, the first signs of patriarchy came in the Neolithic Era (10,200 B.C.E. to between 4,500 and 2,000 B.C.E.). When land got divided, women were forced to remain virgins before marriage so PMs would know who their offspring were, in order to pass their land on to the "right heirs."

Toward the end of the Neolithic Era, women began to get traded as commodities to produce as many babies as possible to tend the land (the more fertile the commodity, the hotter).

Women's value lay in the reproductive system, and the idea of women being good only because of their womb has progressed even into today's society.

As culture evolved, patriarchal society grew more and more misogynistic. Ancient Greece played a major role in the increase of patriarchal practices. When the ancient Greeks transitioned from aristocracy to democracy, men gained equal rights with one another, while women lost more and more rights. Women who didn't follow their traditional functions faced legal consequences. Women couldn't inherit property, had no legal custody of their children, and became the property of men.[1]

Traditional mythology devalued women even more. Goddesses were prevalent during the Paleolithic Era but were demoted in the Neolithic Era. Gods rose and goddesses fell. As the goddesses fell, the misogyny in patriarchy rose.

Philosophers like Aristotle portrayed women as "morally, intellectually, and physically inferior to men; . . . saw women as the property of men; claimed that women's role in society was to reproduce and serve men in the household; and saw male domination of women as natural and virtuous."[2]

The male-dominated society continued, but during the Elizabethan era, when Elizabeth I became the queen of England in 1558, women's empowerment started to become a thing, even if PMs did everything they could to prevent it.

Yet in the modern era, patriarchal practices showed up even more with the division of labor—where men went to work and women stayed at home to raise the children (pretty similar to when land division happened in Neolithic times). Work was exchanged for dollars, whereas raising families had no monetary value, so women once again were at a disadvantage from a power dynamic. The more men worked and women took care of and raised the next generation, the more women had to rely on men to pay for everything, even food, which kept the women and children controlled. This kept the patriarchy strong and continued to reinforce the masculine mind-set of seeking more power, control, and sex.

POWER   NO POWER

In the early 1900s, women started to come together to figure out how to fight the patriarchy and have since been slowly chipping away at the masculine-dominated groundwork that had been laid since the Neolithic Era, thousands of years ago.

Enter feminism and the feminist movement.

WHAT DOES THE TERM "FEMINISM" ACTUALLY MEAN?

Feminism is defined as "a doctrine or movement that advocates equal rights for women."[3]

Gloria Steinem said, "Feminism simply means complete social and economic equality between men and women."[4] Pretty straightforward, right?

AND WHAT IS THE HISTORICAL CONTEXT OF FEMINISM?

The more we understand the history of the patriarchy and the feminist movement, the more we can reshape the future.

So far there have been three "waves" of feminism that built on each other, and according to some scholars, we are now in the "fourth wave." It's important to read this section carefully so that when you get to the "how do we get everyone loving on each other" part of the chapter, you'll have real context.

The first wave (late 19th and early 20th centuries) was all about a woman's right to vote (the suffrage movement). American women were inspired by Emmeline Pankhurst, who led the women's movement in England in the late 1800s and helped English women gain the right to vote in 1918. She didn't care that she was laughed at or told that she was "insane" by society and even arrested on many occasions for using so-called militant tactics (like hunger strikes and picketing) to fight for this right. (It's funny that society back then called women's peaceful hunger strikes and picketing "militant," when men actually waged all-out wars and killed people brutally—the double standard is adorable, right?) By 1920 women in America finally gained the right to vote too.

(Frustrating sidebar: Did you know that women in some countries still today don't have the right to vote? Unbelievable, right? This cause is important to get behind; we must help change this.)

I will get into the tactics of how I believe we can fight the good fight (peacefully) against the current patriarchal system later in this chapter.

The second wave of feminism (late 1950s to 1980s) was mainly around women furthering the gender-equality movement, specifically gaining the right to work as equals to men. We are still fighting that fight, with women earning lower wages and dealing with things like the "maternal wall" gender bias that links motherhood to a "lack of competence and commitment."[5] (Mothers keep their babies alive and yet are "less competent and committed" than PMs? Hmmmm.) The Gender Bias Learning Project study on maternal wall stereotypes found that, "compared to women with identical resumes but no children, mothers were 79% less likely to be hired, 100% less likely to be promoted, . . . and held to higher performance and punctuality standards." That's interesting, because, as I've previously mentioned, new studies are coming out showing that 64 percent of women are either primary or co-breadwinners, women-led companies (including companies led by mothers) are now outperforming male-led companies, and the more that women sit on boards, the more likely those companies are to be successful[6]—so clearly things will level out as concrete data with factual evidence continues to pour in.

The third wave of feminism (1990s) was all about growing the intersectional feminism movement: the notion that feminism stems from something deeper than just "being a woman" and that it is actually more nuanced—like being a "woman of color," or a "gay woman," a "trans woman," a "nonbinary person," or a "woman of a religious or spiritual denomination." The branches of feminism started to grow in different directions here, and some challenges came out of this, like conflicts about which branch was more important than the others. Some would argue that this is when the "feminist catfights" began. Rather than the movement being about all women coming together to cohesively demand equal rights with men, it became an internal war among women to feel seen and understood by each other. Feminism is meant to be inclusive of all races, sexual expressions, gender identities, and lifestyles, so valuing any one of these over another is inherently hypocritical. It's on us to catch ourselves in judgment of others.

We are now in the fourth wave of feminism, said to be about the "women's movement connected through technology."[7] So many more ideas can be transmitted and spread around the world with a simple click of the mouse, so the various feminist movements are scaling up exponentially through technology.

I believe that with technology, we're in a really good place to disseminate new ideas and spread new evidence that supports and strengthens the feminist movement to live in harmony with good men (called SNAGs—secure New-Age guys—more on this in Chapter 12). As feminism is about gender equality, we need good men to be a part of this conversation to truly disrupt the status quo.

WHAT DO YOU SAY WHEN SOMEONE ASKS IF YOU ARE A FEMINIST?

I always start by saying, "What's so great about feminism is that it is meant to be completely inclusive, which gives me the space to define it for myself." By saying something like that, you are giving yourself full freedom to really decide what kind of "feminist" you want to be and gently shutting others down from judging the kind of feminist you are.

Feminism isn't solely defined by feminist books read or feminist T-shirts worn. My feminism is about taking tangible action and creating products and movements that serve and empower all types of women.

YET CAN YOU DO FEMINISM THE WRONG WAY (AKA ABUSE IT)? YES, YOU CAN!

Controversial blogger Janet Bloomfield wrote a piece against fake feminists who tout themselves as feminists but act hypocritically. She said: "As an outspoken critic of feminism, I have quite a bit of experience interacting, both online and IRL [in real life], with feminists, who tend not to take even the mildest criticism of their ideology kindly."[8] The very nature of feminism is meant to be inclusive, and yet "faux feminists" are the first to oppress others (both women and men) who oppose their viewpoints. I believe this has to do with some women being equally as trapped in patriarchal thinking as PMs, and they feel the need to oppress others in order to have any sense of worth.

It also seems that in some cases, feminism is being used as a weapon for retaliation or personal gain. People know when someone screams "feminism," it can sometimes galvanize the social justice warriors, who love standing on their soapboxes. This could be taken advantage of, and we need to watch out for it.

My recommendation? Catch yourself when judging other women for having their own definitions of feminism and stop yourself before using feminism for personal gain or to try to win an argument. This kind of behavior defeats the whole point of the feminist movement. If you love women in the way you say you do, embrace inclusivity with integrity—because that's what feminism is all about.

OPPRESSION ACTUALLY GOES FAR BEYOND GENDER

My friend "Bricky" shared a powerful story with me; it went something like this:

Picture a classroom. It's got six rows of desks, and the teacher's desk is in front. The teacher takes a wastebasket, puts it on his desk in front of the class, and then hands blank pieces of paper to the students. He instructs the students to scrunch the paper into a ball. Then he says that he'll give prizes to the students who can throw the scrunched-up paper into the wastebasket while seated at their desks. The kids in the back get pissed and complain that it will be much harder for them to throw the paper into the basket than for the kids in the front row.

Now imagine the class is divided by gender, race, social class, ethnicity, nationality, sexual orientation, religion, age, mental disability, physical disability, and the like. Generally able-bodied, cisgendered, straight, educationally advantaged white boys are in the front of the class, and other people of various oppressed backgrounds are scattered about the back. It will always be harder for these people in the back to make the basket. They simply must work much harder to gain the privilege of those in the front row.

As this example depicts, yes, women have been dealt a tougher hand than men, but "oppression" goes far beyond gender. All parts of oppression are challenges to overcome.

The intersecting axes of privilege, domination, and oppression show this very clearly:

- Female versus male

- Disabled versus able-bodied

- Uneducated versus educated

- LGBTQ versus heterosexual

- Nonwhite versus white

- Non-native English speaker versus native English speaker

- Unattractive versus attractive

- Old versus young

Gender is only one single point of oppression.

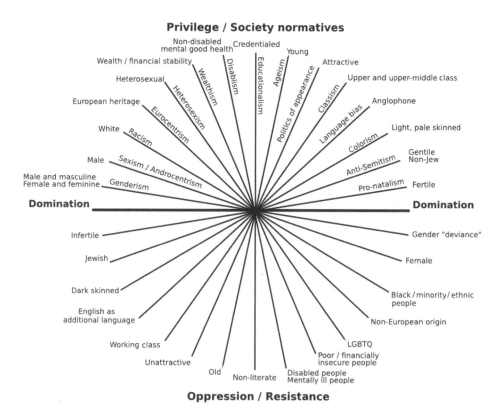

DISRUPT-HER

The hope here is that we can move beyond just female outrage and come together with all oppressed groups and create a tactical plan of action to collectively challenge the current patriarchal system that doesn't authentically support full equality.

WHERE DO WE GO FROM HERE?

The hope of this book is to disrupt status-quo thinking for women in today's patriarchal system, and men should be given permission to get out of it too. The patriarchal system has been in place since the Neolithic Era; perhaps today men want to be liberated from the patriarchy as much as women do.

Psychologist Ronald F. Levant listed the stereotypical norms of the "male sex role,"[9] and these norms clearly demonstrate how trapped men themselves are in the patriarchy:

- Avoiding femininity

- Restrictive emotionality

- Seeking achievement and status

- Aggression

- Homophobia

- Non-relational attitudes toward sexuality

THE MASK OF MASCULINITY

Did men start out wanting to control, dominate, and be restricted emotionally? Doubtful. Men are forced to put on a MASK of MASCulinity of societally acceptable male behaviors that do not allow them to fully express themselves. They are not free to be exactly who they are, and it's on us to help remove the mask with them.

Asked to give up the true self in order
to realize the patriarchal ideal, boys learn
self-betrayal early and are rewarded
for these acts of soul murder.

BELL HOOKS

When you really think about it, men haven't been taught the language of emoting because it's perceived as a sign of weakness. They were taught to care about control, domination, and power and that they were defined by what they *do*.

Imagine a baby trying to share what he is feeling but not having the words to say it, so he can only cry out loud in frustration. Or imagine trying to compete in a race without any developed muscles. This is actually not that different from men who are stuck in the patriarchy without having learned the vocabulary to emote. PMs have not been able to grow the empathetic, feeling side of themselves, so anytime they feel something, it gets bottled up inside until it explodes as violence or anger. Studies have shown that it is more societally acceptable for men to be violent than emotional. PMs also often feel like they don't have permission to be loving (aka "too mushy") or share feelings (aka "acting like a girl") and actually are the ones who commit the most crimes or die most often by suicide because they are so wound up inside.

Doesn't it seem like everyone is kinda trapped in the patriarchy? PMs are stuck wearing the mask of masculinity and women also feel forced to wear it in business. It seems like everyone is out of alignment, all because of masculine notions that were put in place in Neolithic times. Feels like a good time to disrupt all of this, yes?

HOW DO WE GET PMs TO REALIZE THEY CAN CHANGE?

We have a clear understanding of how men stuck in the patriarchy operate today. For example, we know that right now the way PMs often banter is by "talkin' smack" (aka "bro talk"). This is their societally accepted form of intimacy and playfulness.

Women sometimes can make men who show emotions feel weak too.

*"How can you support **me** and be strong for **me** when you are the one being all emotional?"* some women say to men.

Just like men have to catch themselves saying things that put the female gender down, like "you're such a pussy," or "stop acting like a little bitch," or "what a twat," or "mother fucker," or "you throw like a girl," women have to catch themselves saying things like "man up" and "grow some balls" and "you're a dick," which equally oppresses men and make them feel like they cannot show emotions or signs of love, fear, sadness, or any vulnerability at all. If a man is emotional, his partner needs to make him feel safe and held while he emotes. (And if none of this bothers you, then great too!)

A lot of this book is about actively questioning and catching ourselves doing things that we've been conditioned to do and to be fully present to everything we say and do moving forward. It might seem hard at first, but the more we practice catching ourselves doing and saying things that are not in line with who we are, the more true to ourselves and actualized we will become.

In her book *The Will to Change*, bell hooks wrote brilliantly:

> To create loving men, we must love males. Loving maleness is different from praising and rewarding males for living up to sexist-defined notions of male identity. Caring about men because of what they do for us is not the same as loving males for simply being. When we love maleness, we extend our love whether males are performing or not. Performance is different from simply being. In patriarchal culture males are not allowed simply to be who they are and to glory in their unique identity. Their value is always determined by what they do. In an antipatriarchal culture males do not have to prove their value and worth. They know from birth that simply being gives them value, the right to be cherished and loved.[10]

THE FUTURE IS NOT "FEMALE," IT'S FEMININE!

I've been seeing a lot of women wearing "The future is female" T-shirts, which is confusing to me, because it's promoting exactly what women are fighting against: gender oppression. By saying "the future is female," we are still excluding men, which means we are still in the "us against them" mind-set. And as we have learned throughout this book, the way to fight back is not by puffing our chest out at men and saying, "Oh yeah? You excluded us for so long; now it's *your* turn"; it's by going at it differently; it's by including good men in the conversation, men who also see a world where men and women are equal; it's by choosing good men to mate with who see and respect women for who we are.

Therefore, I am replacing the word "female" on those T-shirts with "feminine": "The future is feminine." Feminine includes men, because the feminine exists in all women and men. The feminine exposes our kind, loving, receiving sides. Being "feminine" is truly the opposite of being "weak"; it shows a deep balance within every human.

HOW DO WE PUT THIS ALL INTO PRACTICE?

We are starting to slowly remove the mask of masculinity in today's current patriarchal system, but for now, women *still* need to have an easy system to deal with PMs—and I call it the Triple-Q technique:

1. **Q1: QUIP BACK.** Have your funny quips ready so you're not triggered by PMs.

2. **Q2: QUESTION.** Question them through emotional, vulnerable language, which is hard for PMs. For instance, "Why do you say that?" and "How does that make you feel when you say that?"

3. **Q3: QUIT.** Float away kindly with "This really isn't serving me, or you. I think we should end this interaction and come back together when we're less triggered." Stop PMs in their tracks when they are trying to gain power negatively.

This technique allows women to not play into PMs' strengths but to play into feminine strengths.

Q1: "I QUIPPED BACK."

Start by having fun with it. The way for women to not get intimidated by the current system is to stand up for ourselves in a fun way and not take things as emotionally as we normally would. Instead quip back with funny one-liners. The female pilot from an earlier chapter who didn't land the plane perfectly could say, "What do you mean? That wasn't my fault, it was the ASS-fault." (Get it, "asphalt"? Okay, #momjoke.)

While we are slowly but surely unraveling ourselves from the patriarchal system, it's important for women to first try to meet PMs where they are. By quipping back and joking around with PMs to start with (please just go with me here), women will likely gain their trust and then be able to teach them the new ways of being *faster*— showing them that sharing emotions and authentic feelings is not weakness but true strength and so is respecting women as equals.

Whole Foods is a great example of this.

"If you're such a staunch vegan, then why aren't your stores vegan?"

I was sitting and chatting with my dear friend John Mackey, founder and C.E.O. of Whole Foods Market, in his beautiful Austin home.

"My first store was vegetarian. We didn't sell sugar, white flour, alcohol, or caffeine or meat of any kind. We were very pure and we did almost no business. We were too far ahead of where the market was back in 1978, and we had to evolve to meet the market where we found it or go out of business. I learned at an early age that 'the perfect is the enemy of the good.' Also, we are now over $17 billion in sales and will likely top $18 billion in 2019."

By meeting people where they were, he was able to change millions *more* hearts and minds *faster* to adopt a whole-food, mostly plant-based diet.

It's the same idea with women changing the hearts and minds of men who are stuck firmly in the patriarchy.

If women are constantly getting "outraged" and having hurt feelings "caused by men," then they will always get stuck in the patriarchal system, because men will invariably stick together to fight back. **The current patriarchal stance will be strengthened as a result of female outrage.** Similarly, Whole Foods Market would likely not be a $16 billion company if it had been constantly outraged by the fact that the majority of people ate meat and didn't want to adopt a vegetarian diet.

Another example is where we are in the political climate. The more the left is outraged by the right, the more the right is strengthened and becomes even more united to fight back, and vice versa. **Outrage only creates a further divide**, instead of extending an olive branch to the other side (who also may be exposed to only one way of thinking).

So it's clear that in today's environment, the best way to change hearts and minds as women is to first meet PMs where they are by "quipping back" with a smile on our face, and then educate them once we're "in."

In order to let whatever offense bounce off you so you're able to respond productively, practice being the Warrior Gatekeeper of your mind, catching what's being thrown at you and choosing to not internalize it, and do it playfully. If you know that the line of work you have chosen is very male dominated, you will need to get extra ready, with one-liners already up your sleeve.

Most importantly, when people tease us or attempt to take us down, we have a choice as to how we react. If we get riled up, they will keep coming after us. Look at some people in the media—they will go after the people who get caught by the bullets being shot at them and leave the people who dodge them calmly (think Neo in *The Matrix*) alone.

So ready yourself to receive negative comments by preparing a stash of lighthearted quips. And do everything in your power to have fun with it! Enlist your friends. Really, laugh at it, treat this "serious" matter like a funny game—how many quips can you say before the other person is stumped? Take an improv class (like the ones Upright Citizens Brigade offers) if you need to in order to get that part of your brain firing.

If you don't have a good come-back-y demeanor initially when men are egging you on, you'll likely be the one picked on.

If you come back with a good one-liner, more than likely they will start to build a bridge with you and say, "Okay, this girl can take it after all."

The less you let them get under your skin, the less they'll be inclined to make fun of you, because it's not getting a rise out of you.

And then your work can begin to let them understand how to tap into the deeper side of themselves and feel safe enough to start emoting differently.

"So wait, how did you make them stop being jerks?"

"I just quipped back, and they stopped and have since become much more respectful."

Q2: IF PLAYFUL QUIPS DON'T WORK, TIME TO QUESTION THEM

If your jokes, quips, and one-liners don't work, and PMs still don't stop bullying or teasing you, you can then move on to the next Q: turning the tables on them with questions.

Asking questions that target their emotional intelligence is a great way to open them up to the side of themselves that they have not been allowed to tap into.

- "How did that make you feel when you said that?"

- "What is the positive take-away here?"

- "I understand that you're stressed, but is there a reason you're taking it out on me? I'm trying to help here."

- "Is everything okay? Is there something else you are feeling that I can help you with?"

Seems silly, but PMs are likely not used to women standing up for themselves and turning the negative emotions back on them like that with a powerful question, so they often get uncomfortable, and some might see what they have done or said as not great. Some might pound their chest here and try to deflect whatever is wrong back onto you, and this is where you cannot get triggered or get emotional and cry. Stand strong!

"So wait, how did you make him stop being an asshole?"

"I questioned him."

Q3: IF PLAYFUL QUIPS AND QUESTIONING THEM DON'T WORK, TIME TO QUIT THE MOMENT

This is where you really stop PMs in their tracks when they are trying to overpower you and your funny remarks and questions just didn't do the trick.

A woman in a board room was being put down ruthlessly by a PM and she literally stood up, calmly pointed to the door, and said, "I'd like to start this conversation over respectfully. Can we all walk back into the room and start over with respect?" The key word here is "calmly."

Another way to say it:

"This really isn't serving either of us. I think we should end this interaction and come back together when we're less triggered."

If you get to the point of QUITTING the moment, it's important for you to know that the PM might again puff his chest out even more to fight back, and this is where you can enlist other people to support you, like HR, friends, or peers.

But start playfully with funny quips and escalate from there as needed. The best way to get PMs to change their behavior and disrupt the status quo is through the least resistance initially, intensifying thereafter if necessary. It's much better (and more fun) to extend a hand instead of punching someone in the face first.

It's crazy to think that we have been wearing masks all this time. It make sense because it's been hard to navigate societal conditioning and peer pressure, all while trying to be authentically ourselves. Even if you might think, "I don't want to kowtow to the current patriarchal system and play *their* game," we *do* have to face the fact that this is the current reality that we live in, so we may as well have fun with it and try and get PMs to change their hearts and minds through a fun game (aka Triple-Q technique) instead of starting with anger right off the bat.

It's truly time to get back to being unapologetically WHO WE ARE in our most authentic, fun, human form. Again, for emphasis, the more we can have fun with it and not be so bothered by "how it should be" (whether we are justified or not), and let it all be a fun sport to play, the more those who are stuck in the old ways will open themselves up to actually changing themselves for the better.

PUTTING IT ALL TOGETHER

To be a Disrupt-Her, you must (1) get back to your childlike state of curiosity, playfulness, and awe; (2) practice addition by subtraction in all facets of your life; (3) figure out what your LIT path is as opposed to a traditional "career path"; (4) start investing your money wisely; (5) become a Warrior Gatekeeper of your mind by actively catching what comes to your mental gate (and then practicing pattern interruption if you do accidentally let in a negative thought and start spiraling out of control); (6) iterate and get better every day in all the things you're doing, instead of focusing on being perfect; (7) catch yourself when you're being a Hate-Her by understanding where you are in your life personally and where you are not in integrity; (8) embody your inner Disrupt-Her unapologetically; and (9) truly define feminism for yourself.

DISRUPTION #9

EXERCISES

1. Define the word "feminist" for yourself. Please don't just talk and troll; instead join movements in a positive way and encourage women (and men) to be inclusive.

2. When you see PMs trapped behind the mask of masculinity, don't write them off. Understand that they have not been given permission to develop the "muscles" to show emotions and everything is bottled up inside. They are suffering as much as you are. You are not excusing PMs for oppressing women and others, and you will stand up to that, but by understanding their inner turmoil, you might feel more inclined to include them when we disrupt the patriarchal system and liberate all humans from it, including men.

3. When dealing with PMs in their current climate, practice managing them using the Triple-Q technique.

4. Catch yourself when you say or think things that are of the patriarchal mind-set—like "Grow some balls" or "Man up!" or "You're unsexy when you cry"—and catch yourself when your man is attempting to be emotional and you write him off or laugh at him or find him unattractive. Encourage new learned behavior.

5. Call men out when they say things like, "Stop acting like a bitch" or "mother fucker" or "he was a total sissy." Try not to lead with outrage—quip back first and escalate from there.

RB ACCOUNTABILIBUDDY
ACTION #9!

ISN'T IT FUN TO HELP PEOPLE
REVEAL WHO THEY REALLY ARE?!

NOW THAT WE RECOGNIZE THAT PMs ARE TRAPPED BEHIND
THE MASK OF MASCULINITY AND WOMEN ARE OPPRESSED
BY IT TOO, HAVING TO RESORT TO FEMINIST OUTRAGE,
WE GET TO NOW TAKE THE STEPS TO HELP REMOVE
THE MASK AND ALLOW EVERYONE'S TRUEST SELVES TO EMERGE.
ONCE MEN CAN FEEL SAFE EMOTING AND FEELING THINGS
LIKE PAIN, SADNESS, AND LOVE, THEY WILL LIKELY
NO LONGER FEEL THE NEED TO CONTROL, DOMINATE,
AND OVERPOWER TO NUMB THEIR LACK OF FEELING
OR BLOW UP VIOLENTLY FROM PENT-UP ANGUISH.
THE MORE WOMEN AND MEN ARE ABLE TO EXPRESS
THEMSELVES AUTHENTICALLY AND WITH INTEGRITY,
THE FASTER WE WILL HEAL FROM THE PAST.
FEMINISM AND THE PATRIARCHY WILL BE THINGS
WE FIND IN HISTORY BOOKS.

WHENEVER YOU FEEL LIKE YOU ARE TRAPPED IN THE PATRIARCHY,
RB IS ASKING YOU TO TAKE HER OFF YOUR RIGHT WRIST
AND PUT HER ON YOUR LEFT WRIST (JUST FOR THIS EXERCISE).
NOW PRETEND YOU ARE WEARING A MASK AND PRETEND TO REMOVE IT.
PUTTING RB ON YOUR OTHER WRIST REMINDS YOU THAT THINGS
DON'T HAVE TO STAY THE WAY THEY ALWAYS HAVE BEEN.
FEEL YOUR REAL SELF
EMERGING.

AND WHENEVER SOMEONE ELSE
IS ACTING OUT IN A PATRIARCHAL,
DOMINATING WAY, PRETEND
THEY ARE WEARING A MASK AND
THEN PRETEND TO REMOVE IT.

THEY'LL BE CONFUSED BY WHAT YOU'RE DOING (FEEL FREE TO
TELL THEM), BUT RB WILL BE THERE TO KEEP YOU COMPANY.
SHE WILL HELP REMIND YOU THAT BEING OUTRAGED
BY THEIR MASK OF MASCULINITY WON'T CHANGE ANYONE.
AND SHE'LL HELP YOU GET INTO THE
TRIPLE-Q TECHNIQUE **RIGHT AWAY.**

DISRUPTION #10

Don't be emotional in business.

We can expose every side of ourselves powerfully, both in our business and in our personal lives.

"I can't see and I can't breathe. It's too hot in here."

My heart started palpitating a mile a minute, and my brain started looking for an "abort mission" plan.

My girlfriend Elana had invited me to a sweat lodge ceremony at Esalen, in Big Sur, California, with a group of badass female leaders in a tepee, and my claustrophobic brain started screaming at me as soon as the chief closed the door to the tepee, making it pitch black in the tiny, confined space. I felt like I was inhaling ten packs of cigarettes all at once. (I can only assume, because I've actually never smoked a cigarette in my life. I'm one of those people who would look SO goofy smoking a cigarette.)

The women to the left and right of me clasped my hands tightly to give me comfort, and as I felt their bodies relax, I tried to relax mine too, but my brain was *still* in the *get-me-the-hell-outta-here* panic phase.

How on earth has NOT ONE woman left this damn tepee yet? said the voice in my head. The only thing that had kept me there up to this point was my competitive spirit—I didn't want to be the first one to fold.

Fuck it. I couldn't take it anymore. I was just about to spring up and out when. . .

"Earth my body,
water my blood,
air my breath,
and fire my spirit."

Jess Magic (yes, that's her name), started singing a beautiful, haunting chant, and all the women in the tepee followed suit. Her tone was stable and sweet, strong and sensual all at the same time.

Somehow the singing distracted me from the *I'm-gonna-die-if-I-stay-here-for-one-more-second* exodus moment and I joined in.

And then I transcended.

From fear to divine strength.

The strength of 20 women stuffed in a tepee chanting for dear life as our skin seared off.

I jest—though it was actually one of the most powerful experiences I've ever had. As we chanted these lyrics over and over, not one of us left the dark, smoky hut. I got to the place of getting past my ego, my fight-or-flight brain, my physical self, my fears, my worries, and the patriarchy. I hit a reset state.

The goal of a sweat lodge ceremony is for Native Americans to purify themselves and repair damage done to their spirit, mind, and body.

"With the introduction of alcohol and the inhumane treatment of native people, the need to re-purify themselves and find their way back to traditional ways of living became evident, as they were becoming increasingly poisoned by European culture."[1]

Kinda perfect for women to purify in a similar way from a very patriarchal, masculine world, right?

Two things happened during and after this experience:

The first was that I felt an undeniable sisterhood that a person can only feel from going through a life-and-death experience like this one (it felt life-and-death for me, anyway) with other women. Strong women joined hands and joined breath and overcame the external and internal obstacles *together*. There was no separateness; this was a circle of women transcending together. I felt the strength of ancient mothers coming together to hold us to our highest selves and move through the terrifying experience gracefully.

I was so awakened by this experience that it unlocked more in me that day.

Some might say I felt my "Shakti."

Shakti is the Hindu goddess that represents supreme feminine power. My Indian father has been teaching me about Shakti via the Hindu scriptures called the Mahabharata and the Ramayana since I was a child, and my girlfriend Elana has been reorbiting the concept around me for a while, and it all finally clicked.

Shakti can be further defined as "dynamic energy that is responsible for creation, maintenance, and destruction of the universe. It is identified as female energy because shakti is responsible for creation, as mothers are responsible for birth. Without shakti, nothing in this universe would happen."[2]

Shakti also embodies the "Supreme Goddess," and she manifests as various goddess forms. (I know this sounds woo-woo, but I bring it back to reality shortly, so stick with this, please.) For example, she could manifest as the gentle and nurturing Parvati, goddess of fertility, love, and devotion. Or she could manifest as Kali, who is equal parts terrifying force that destroys evil and a powerful mother figure, or as Durga, the invincible warrior who conquers forces that threaten the stability of the universe.[3] Or she could manifest as Lalita ("she who plays"), goddess of bliss and sensuality. Or Saraswati, goddess of wisdom and learning. Or Lakshmi, goddess of wealth and well-being.

When Shakti is fully embodied, she can be all the powerful goddesses at once.

BRINGING THIS BACK TO REALITY

In today's patriarchal world, women are not given permission to be fully embodied. That is, we can't be gentle, nurturing, loving, devoted, a terrifying force, powerful, an invincible warrior, and a wise, wealthy, and playfully sensual mother figure all at the same time. We have been placed in a one-dimensional either-or box. Either we are a gentle, nurturing, loving, devoted mother figure OR we are a powerful, invincible, warriorlike, wealth-creating businesswoman. And being sensual is a whole other thing. It's also hard for society to let us feel both nurturing and sensual at the same time. We're all forced to allow only a certain socially acceptable side of ourselves to appear based on what we do in the world (entrepreneur, businesswoman, stay-at-home mom, artist, musician, creative, etc.).

In the world of business, I have been taught that the only way to get ahead is to play the role of Durga, the warrior. It was pretty easy for me to tap into this because I was an athlete and that side of myself was more available to me. Bringing out my warrior side helped drive my businesses forward and helped me raise money, but I forgot about the other important sides of myself, and that created an imbalance in me. And men have to wear their warrior masks all the time without exposing the rest of themselves, resulting in an imbalance in the world too, an imbalance that makes them less loving, nurturing, and emotionally available . . .

. . . which brings me to my second experience at Esalen, post–sweat lodge adventure.

I was surging with so much released energy from the sweat lodge that I went back to my cabin by myself, locked the door, took all my clothes off, and . . .

. . . danced in front of the mirror seductively by myself for a full hour, without any music, completely sober. I literally seduced myself for an hour. It was both weird and liberating all at once.

My Lalita goddess emerged in full force. I couldn't even control the motions of my seductive dance in the mirror, it just happened. And I let it.

I gave myself full permission to be sensual . . . for myself, and not for anyone else.

And for someone who still had to operate in business in this current realm, it was truly LIBERATING.

Just like men have not developed the muscles to emote, I hadn't developed the muscles to allow the other parts of myself to be fully manifested. Until that moment when my inner sensual Lalita came out, I had kept her quite hidden and felt generally uncomfortable being overtly sexy, especially as a businesswoman. My tomboy was far more prevalent, because it was easier to fit in that way and get ahead with the boys and operate within the patri-archal system. Being sensual and sexy was threatening in society, so it was better kept hidden. I realized that I loved intimate time with my partner because I longed for my Lalita to come out. She was hidden in the outer-facing world, and the only time she came out was in the bedroom, so it made sense that I craved intimate time. If we let our fully embodied selves emerge in all facets of our lives, imagine how much more balanced we would be every day and how much more connected to one another and to the planet we would be as a result.

As I recently became a mother, I felt my inner Parvati come out in full force. I've never been so devoted or nurturing like this before, and I let this side of myself stretch out so I could feel it fully. Before internalizing the full spectrum of myself, I would have still remained in the Durga warrior hamster wheel of business to grow, grow, grow, and push, push, push, even while pregnant and after giving birth, but instead I gave myself permission to fully embody the nurturing Parvati and relax into it during and after the birth.

During pregnancy I also felt my inner Kali, the mother figure who destroys evil (terrifyingly), come out. I felt myself completely lose tolerance for those who are not in full integrity and for unconscious people in business who take advantage of others.

Everything became crystal clear.

And I didn't fight it. Any of it.

I didn't fight my natural womanly instincts to be every version of myself unapologetically. I felt my capacity to empathize grow, and I loved how this newly expanded me made me show up in the world, with more presence and resonance within myself. No hiding the quirky, the sensual, the fun-loving, the childlike, the motherly, the spirited versions of myself—everything was available when I felt them. *Ahhhhhh! I can breathe!*

Now the goal is to figure out how to replace the only acceptable manifestation of Shakti in the current business world (Durga the warrior) with a multilayered, fully embodied Shakti goddess to run the show. Imagine: if fully embodied women (and men) ran the business world in a safe space, what would it look like? Conscious businesses would become ubiquitous. Being loving and nurturing in business would not be an outlier anymore.

I sit on the board of Conscious Capitalism Inc. (CCI) with several badass founders and C.E.O.s of major businesses like Whole Foods, the Container Store, Grameen Bank, Trader Joe's, Jamba Juice, and Hotels.com, among several others, and the goal of Conscious Capitalism is to show the world that consciously led businesses *can* change the world for the better.

Conscious Capitalism is based on four principles:

1. **HIGHER PURPOSE**—focusing on meaning and purpose over profit: "Purpose activates us and motivates us. It moves us to get up in the morning, sustains us when times get tough and serves as a guiding star when we stray off course."

2. **STAKEHOLDER ORIENTATION**—focusing on all stakeholders: "Without employees, customers, suppliers, funders, supportive communities and a life-sustaining ecosystem, there is no business. Conscious Business is a win-win-win proposition, which includes a healthy return to shareholders."

3. **CONSCIOUS LEADERSHIP**—"Conscious Leaders focus on 'we,' rather than 'me.' They inspire, foster transformation and bring out the best in those around them."

4. **CONSCIOUS CULTURE**—"Culture is the embodied values, principles and practices underlying the social fabric of a business, which permeate its actions and connects the stakeholders to each other and to the company's purpose, people and processes."[4]

This way of doing business allows all sides of the Shakti goddess to emerge. And it's proving to outperform all major stock indexes by several multiples. So, in fact, allowing the abundant Shakti mind-set to emerge is actually *better financially* than the scarcity patriarchal mind-set with which most current business is conducted across the world.

As the newest member of the board, I spent most of my time observing the rest of the board and how they ran the board meetings. I was so moved by the way they treated the C.E.O. with nurturing love, lifted him up when he struggled, and consciously put him into different courses to strengthen his less-developed skill sets.

I'll never forget sitting in a CCI board meeting and listening to the members discuss their feelings so openly.

"I felt hurt when you said _____."

"Let's examine the energy in the room"

"I'd love to send some love to X board member for doing Y."

"I feel really sad that you said _____."

The people around the table were leaders of multibillion-dollar enterprises and talking in "I feel" statements almost the entire time. It was a whole new way of thinking about business, allowing for the nurturing Parvati, the wise Saraswati, and the well-being-conscious Lakshmi to come out. When the CCI C.E.O. didn't hit his projected numbers, instead of the board being frustrated, they said, "We have made progress compared to last year, so let's keep the wind in his sails and encourage him to keep going," and "We must be patient and give him time. It's like flowers, you can't just pull flowers out of the ground and look at the roots every day to see how they're doing, you have to give them time to grow and get stronger on their own, but with our love and care." It's no wonder the companies that these board members are a part of are absolutely THRIVING.

I have since spent time with my TUSHY team consciously working through setting up core values early on, creating rituals like Friday Props (giving special shout-outs to team members who kicked ass that week), making sure we have monthly team outings, like going to Daybreaker and getting fun meals together. Our relationships with suppliers, vendors, and investors are better than ever, and we are not a "top-down" organization (I realized people could take advantage of this structure) but one based on everyone's "zone of genius."[5]

I saw that the top-down model didn't work well for the type of people I wanted to attract, so I changed TUSHY to a "zone of genius" model—which basically means that each person is the leader within their own expertise (whether marketing, operations, creative, content, development, etc.). This way, each individual can truly own their department. It then becomes about hiring the absolute best people for each role and letting them work their magic and take ownership of their space.

For example, Justin (you met him earlier, remember) is the best operations person on the TUSHY team, so everyone follows his lead on everything operations. Andy is the best digital marketing person on the team, so everyone follows his lead on all things digital marketing. Corin is the best content person on the team, so everyone follows her lead on content. I love the creative aspect of the business, so I run creative. No one person is seen as "higher up" than another; everyone owns what they're great at and gets recognized for it, everyone trusts each other's leadership within their own departments, and nobody is more exposed than another. It works on all levels.

If fully embodied humans could create a fully embodied company culture, I wasn't ever going back.

PUTTING IT ALL TOGETHER

To be a Disrupt-Her, you must (1) get back to your childlike state of curiosity, playfulness, and awe; (2) practice addition by subtraction in all facets of your life; (3) figure out what your LIT path is as opposed to a traditional "career path"; (4) start investing your money wisely; (5) become a Warrior Gatekeeper of your mind by actively catching what comes to your mental gate (and then practicing pattern interruption if you do accidentally let in a negative thought and start spiraling out of control); (6) iterate and get better every day in all the things that you're doing, instead of focusing on being perfect; (7) catch yourself when you're being a Hate-Her by understanding where you are in your life personally and where you are not in integrity; (8) embody your inner Disrupt-Her unapologetically; (9) define feminism for yourself, and help men remove their masks of masculinity using the Triple-Q technique and by loving and supporting them when they show their emotional side; and (10) give yourself full permission to expose ALL your Shakti goddesses in business and in life, find your zone of genius at work, and help your workplace become a conscious business through the Conscious Capitalism principles.

DISRUPTION #10

EXERCISES

1. Can you find and describe all sides of yourself based on the Shakti goddesses?

2. Which goddess do you feel that you are most connected to and that is out in the world?

3. Which goddess are you hiding and not growing?

4. How can the business you work in become a conscious business based on the Conscious Capitalism principles?

5. What are the zones of genius within your team?

6. What kind of fun, creative, unique core values can you create with your team that ALL sides of yourself can stand behind?

**GET TO KNOW
ALL YOUR GODDESSES!**

IT'S SO FUN TO
DISCOVER AND
EXPLORE ALL SIDES
OF OURSELVES,
ISN'T IT?!
I T'S LIKE KNOWING
THAT SOME OF
OUR MUSCLES ARE
STRONGER THAN OTHERS,
SO NOW IT'S TIME TO WORK OUT
THE WEAKER ONES
AND GET THE ENTIRE BODY
STRONG AND WHOLE!

ISN'T IT FUN TO THINK ABOUT THE DIFFERENT SIDES
OF OURSELVES AS "GODDESSES" AND RECOGNIZE
WHICH ONES WE SHOW IN THE WORLD AND
WHICH ONES WE KEEP HIDDEN DEEP INSIDE?

YOU MIGHT
FEEL SUPER UNCOMFORTABLE
AND GOOFY TAKINGTHIS ACTION,
BUT THIS IS YOUR OPPORTUNITY TO REALLY SHOW UP
FOR YOURSELF WITHOUT ANY JUDGMENT.
RB IS ASKING YOU TO RECORD YOURSELF
TAKING HER OFF AND DANCING IN FRONT OF THE MIRROR,
TWIRLING RB IN YOUR HAND.
GET TO KNOW YOUR INNER **LALITA!**
AND THEN WATCH THE VIDEO.
THE GOAL HERE IS THAT NOTHING YOU DO SHOULD WEIRD
YOURSELF OUT, BECAUSE YOU'RE THAT COMFORTABLE
THAT YOU CAN DO ANYTHING WITH YOURSELF.
THAT GODDESS IS IN YOU; SHE JUST NEEDS
TO BE INVITED TO COME OUT.
YOUR ACCOUNTABILIBUDDY RB IS GIVING YOU
FULL PERMISSION TO
SHOW ALL OF YOURSELF TO THE WORLD.
WATCH AND FEEL YOURSELF BECOMING LIBERATED!

RB ACCOUNTABILIBUDDY
ACTION #10!

DISRUPTION #11

Failure is embarrassing.
Even "failing forward" is embarrassing.

DISRUPTION

Replace the word "failure"
with "revelation."

*The credit belongs to the [wo]man who is actually
in the arena, whose face is marred by dust and sweat
and blood; who strives valiantly; who errs; who comes
short again and again, because there is no effort
without error and shortcoming; but who does actually
strive to do the deeds; who knows great enthusiasms,
the great devotions; who spends [her]self in a worthy
cause; who at the best knows in the end the triumph
of high achievement, and who at the worst, if [s]he fails,
at least fails while daring greatly, so that [her] place
shall never be with those cold and timid souls
who neither know victory nor defeat.*

THEODORE ROOSEVELT

"Please go find the best path for the group to cross the forest," the leader instructed the scout.

The scout took the order from the leader and proceeded calmly and excitedly.

By definition, a scout is "a soldier or person sent out ahead of a main force to explore, examine or gather information about a place, or to do recon."[1]

A scout is one who pushes the boundaries of the unknown, runs into new territory first with excitement and curiosity to uncover new things, and is often first to encounter major pushback from whatever crosses her path (for example, a fallen log that blocks the road, or a ravine that prevents crossing, or hungry bears looking for a human meal). The scout examines the current situation, decides where to go, and strategizes how to get the job done. Most importantly the scout is not afraid to "fail," and actually doesn't understand the word "failure"—the words the scout chooses are "learning" and "growing" and "having revelations."

For example, if the scout who is doing recon for a larger group goes ahead on her own and runs into a ravine she can't cross, does the scout turn back and call herself a "failure" and have an "it's over" mentality, or does she simply turn around and look for a new path?

The scout doesn't ever think of any obstacles or long journeys with dead ends as "failures" or a waste of time. The scout doesn't judge herself for choosing one path over another. She simply learned where not to go next time and saw some cool things on her way to the dead end. She doesn't take the journey so seriously, even if much seems to be at stake.

It's so easy for us all to put negative meaning on the things that take us to dead ends or to beat ourselves up for taking the wrong path at the fork, but it has nothing to do with failing. It has everything to do with learning and growing and having aha moments. It has everything to do with seeing an opportunity to do better the next go-round.

A Disrupt-Her, in essence, is a modern-day scout.

To be a Disrupt-Her requires the ability to see every unknown path ahead as an amazing adventure and a constant stream of revelations.

WOMEN DEALING WITH "FAILURE" IN CURRENT SOCIETY

> A woman who gets a B in a course is likely to drop it, while men persist. . . . Women hold themselves to higher standards and are more quickly discouraged. . . . If women don't succeed, they take it personally. . . . Women can be so afraid of failure that they're disinclined to even try. . . . The second greatest reason why women don't apply for jobs is because they don't want to put themselves in a position to fail. . . . Rather than eagerly searching for opportunities to challenge themselves, women tend to be anchored in their comfort zones. . . . Men will look at a negotiation as the equivalent of going to a ballgame, while women categorize it like going to a dentist.[2]

It's kinda hard not to get a little intimidated (aka conditioned, aka brainwashed) by things like this in the media if you're a woman, right? Most people don't read more than headlines anyway, so if these are the constant messages that women read in the press, that would likely make us internalize them and feel *even more* uncomfortable in trying to PRESS GO!, wouldn't you say? We think things like, *I'd just be proving what's already been proven, so why even attempt at all?*

I have read that women and men have different ways of handling "failure." Men see it as a badge of honor, and women see it as something really shameful.

Based on the headlines, you might think that women really *are* harder on themselves and have a harder time dealing with "failure" than men. But actually it's clear that this mind-set stems from a deeply held patriarchal bias against women rising in the ranks in the workplace. It's not about women's "lack of capabilities" and "fear of failure" or "lack of desire to be competitive," it's actually about the status-quo thinking that is holding women back.

For example, if society is used to having PMs run the finance world and all of a sudden women infiltrate the industry, the current system will do everything it can to push back against any change. So the industry will of course hold women to a higher standard and do whatever is possible to help women "fail." And if women do "fail," PMs make them feel terrible that they made any attempt at all, so that the status quo will remain intact.

According to a Harvard University study, "People who are employed in an occupation that is strongly associated with the opposite gender are penalized more harshly for making mistakes."[3]

Since PMs dominate most industries, women are immediately in a challenging position.

It's natural to feel intimidated before you enter a ring that you've never been in. And women have not been allowed to PRESS GO! for more than a few decades, so there is already more to lose if you do fail.

So it's not just the fear of failing that comes into play here; any risk is also wrapped in real societal thinking that "if you *do* fail, you will be laughed back to the kitchen where you belong."

So making the attempt to PRESS GO! is only *one* part of the "failure hurdle" that women need to overcome. Going against the societal mind-set is the other part.

In order for women to get over both issues, we need to rename the concept of failure. "Failure" is a word that makes people feel bad and scared. Even the concept of "failing forward" doesn't feel great, because it still has the word "failing" in it.

Let's first understand the term "fail" before we replace it.

The definition of "fail" is "to fall short of success or achievement in something expected, attempted, desired, or approved."[4]

When we think about failure in the historical and even cultural context (like in the movies), it's also often the "bad guys" that fail in the end and are disapproved of. In many ways failing = being the bad guy. So it makes sense that people don't want to fail—nobody wants to be the bad guy in the end.

Another reason the word "failure" needs to be replaced is because the concept of failure feels so permanent (not to mention embarrassing!): "It's over. I failed."

There is a real fear of having to start over if things don't work out, so the thought process is, *I may as well stay in my safety net, even if I'm not inspired at all. Because I'd rather stay safe than go for it and risk failing and my life being an embarrassment.*

So we don't go for it. Our ideas, our passion projects, our adventures, the next phases of our LIT path, none of it moves forward because of fear-of-failure paralysis.

But whenever you start thinking about your fear of failure or read anything about failing, remember the SCOUT.

REVELATIONS

We need to realize that "failure" shouldn't even be part of the language when we are making an attempt at creating, launching, or doing something that we love. When we make any attempt at all, we are already growing and learning from the experience, so even if it doesn't succeed the first time, a new opportunity will present itself and we will have a clearer picture of how to do it better the next time.

Let's go ahead and replace the term "failing" with "having a revelation."

So if someone says, "Oh yeah, I heard Sally failed at her start-up," you can then correct them and say, "You mean Sally had a revelation with her start-up?" Meaning, she grew and learned from the experience.

The definition of "REVELATION" fits perfectly as the new "failure" replacement: *"the act of revealing or disclosing; disclosure; something revealed or disclosed, especially a striking disclosure, as of something not before realized."*[5]

Learning and growing has never been about "failure," it's always been about disclosing something not before realized, revealing the truth, and recognizing that all experiences, both good and bad, are part of the growing process.

The more you reveal, the more you'll learn, and the more you'll be able to grow for the next time. Nothing is finite (except life).

MY REVELATIONS

I have certainly had my fair share of revelations while building my businesses! Some were more intense than others, but they were all great learning experiences. For example, I didn't focus on the hiring process as much as I should have in the past, and I had lots of revelations about it thereafter (like "Hire slow, fire fast"!). I launched products that didn't quite fit the market at the moment, and I learned the importance of timing. I launched side businesses that took energy away from my core business, and I learned to focus. I also learned how to be a better leader and manager through challenging experiences.

Do any of those feel like "failures"? No way! (Though they might have at the time. . .) I have always been SO grateful for my revelations, even if sometimes it took me a while to see them.

The universe *does* actually conspire *for* us, even when experiences seem negative.

My friend Amber Rae shared something with me that stuck. She said to try going from:

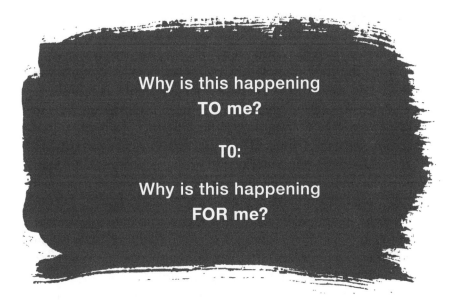

Why is this happening
TO me?

TO:

Why is this happening
FOR me?

I realized that "TO me" promotes victimhood, helplessness, and oftentimes a sense of failure, whereas "FOR me" promotes growth, learning, and having revelations. When you replace that sense of "I failed" with an understanding of "what was revealed to me from this experience," you will be grateful to everyone that participated in the experience.

Having gone through challenging times myself, I became even more inspired to write this book to help women get out of the victimhood and "fear of failure" mentality and into a loving, self-actualized state, free of negative conditioning, patterns, and beliefs.

The more we go through challenging times, the more that is revealed, and the more we get to learn and grow. From that mind-set, only gratitude emerges.

THE POSTMORTEM

"You need to do a postmortem," Lauren, my coach, said.

"You need to write down exactly what happened, what you learned, and what you could have done differently. You need to write down what your vision is for yourself both personally and in business five years from now. By making this postmortem part of the process sacred, you will imprint the lessons you've learned."

I realized how important it is to create a "postmortem" after any revelation happens. To debrief and document what happened clarifies what direction to go next time. For example, if a scout chose to go in a direction that hit a ravine and didn't document the revelation when she came back, she might forget the lesson and hit the ravine again. It's great to revisit your postmortems before making big decisions moving forward.

Also, writing down my vision for myself in business and in my personal life five years from now helped put me in the mental state to EXIST in that vision—to truly BE in that state, knowing that my vision will happen if I just live there. We are all incredible manifesters, and the more we believe, the more we will make aligned choices that will get us where we want to go.

WHAT HAPPENED?

WHAT I LEARNED?

WHAT COULD I HAVE DONE DIFFERENTLY?

A Disrupt-Her will run into roadblocks all the time. She gets that it's all part of the fun game of life and never looks at anything as a "failure" or even "failing forward." The word "fail" doesn't even exist for her. Instead she lives for the many amazing revelations that come her way and looks forward to learning and growing from all of them. If we are all able to see all experiences, both "good" and "bad," as simply interesting, unique experiences, without any charge, without any preconceptions of what they "mean" or "should mean," then we will be forever liberated and excited for the unknown (adventures) ahead.

PUTTING IT ALL TOGETHER

To be a Disrupt-Her, you must (1) get back to your childlike state of curiosity, playfulness, and awe; (2) practice addition by subtraction in all facets of your life; (3) figure out what your LIT path is as opposed to a traditional "career path"; (4) start investing your money wisely; (5) become a Warrior Gatekeeper of your mind by actively catching what comes to your mental gate (and then practicing pattern interruption if you do accidentally let in a negative thought and start spiraling out of control); (6) iterate and get better every day in all the things you're doing, instead of focusing on being perfect; (7) catch yourself when you're being a Hate-Her by understanding where you are in your life personally and where you are not in integrity; (8) embody your inner Disrupt-Her fully and unapologetically; (9) define feminism for yourself, and help men remove their masks of masculinity using the Triple-Q technique and by loving and supporting them when they show their emotional side; (10) give yourself full permission to expose ALL your Shakti goddesses in business and in life; and (11) replace the word "failure" with "revelation" and never skip the postmortem part of the process.

DISRUPTION #11

EXERCISES

1. In what way have you been a "scout" in your life? What was a situation when you ran into a road-block, and how did you handle it?

2. Do a postmortem after each revelation, always. Don't ignore this part; it's extremely important to write things down and figure out what to do next time.

3. We have to be sensitive with words—how to speak about things—the new language is not "failing" but "having revelations."

HOW MUCH MORE FUN
IS THE WORD "REVELATION" THAN "FAILURE"?

IMAGINE IF YOU HAD THE ABILITY TO GO AFTER THE
THING YOU ARE EXCITED ABOUT WITHOUT THE
WHAT IF I FAIL?
THOUGHT RUMBLING THROUGH YOUR BRAIN.
IMAGINE IF YOU GOT TO SAY TO YOURSELF,
WHAT REVELATIONS WILL I HAVE WHEN I PRESS GO?
ON MY DREAMY IDEAS? WHAT WILL I LEARN AND HOW
WILL I GROW FROM THIS EXPERIENCE? AND MOST
IMPORTANTLY, YOU WILL SAY TO YOURSELF WITH A LAUGH,
WHAT IS FAILURE ANYWAY? IN OUR SHORT LIVES,
ALL THE THINGS WE ARE EXPERIENCING ARE JUST THAT:
INTERESTING EXPERIENCES THAT WE GET TO HAVE.
DOESN'T THAT MAKE IT SO MUCH LESS DAUNTING TO
GO AFTER THAT WHICH OUR **HEART DESIRES?**

WHENEVER YOU HAVE THE **WHAT IF I FAIL?**
THOUGHT POP UP IN YOUR HEAD, RB IS ASKING
YOU TO FIRST LAUGH OUT LOUD AND SAY TO YOURSELF
WHAT IS FAILURE, ANYWAY?
WHEN YOU FEEL SOCIETY'S CONDITIONING
AND BELIEF SYSTEMS AROUND "FAILING"
START PILING ON YOU,
RB IS ASKING YOU TO GRAB YOUR EARS
AND MASSAGE THEM.
THIS WILL HELP REMIND YOU THAT
YOU CAN **FLIP YOUR MIND-SET**
FROM "FAILURE" TO "REVELATION" AND TO REMEMBER
THAT ALL EXPERIENCES ARE THRILLING
OPPORTUNITIES TO LEARN AND GROW!

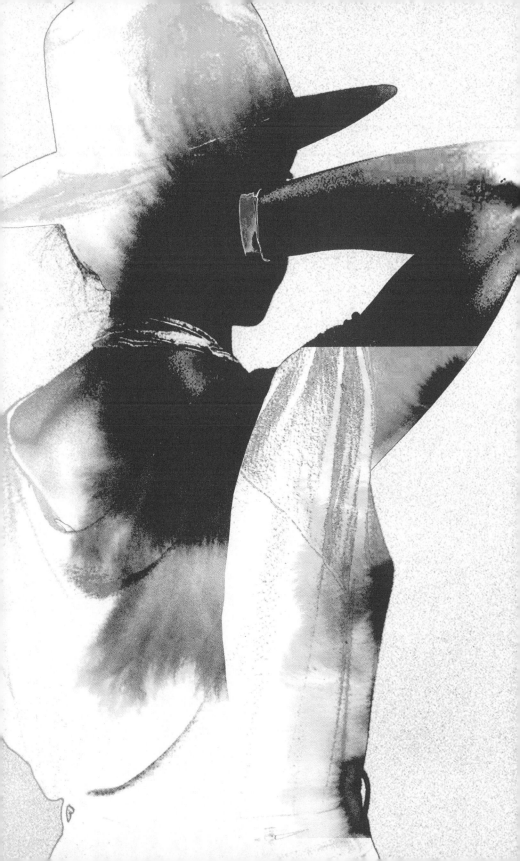

DISRUPTION #12

Don't be picky
when finding a mate.

Breed a SNAG
(Secure New Age Guy or Gal)!

"Wait, I don't understand what's going on."

My mouth was completely agape as I took my blindfold off.

Thirty of my closest friends, all dressed up in white, were standing in a row on either side of me in the middle of a forest.

Andrew and Radha's boyfriend, Eli, were supposed to take Radha and me on a fun weekend adventure filled with surprises, but this was a whole different thing. I had no idea why all my friends were here when it was supposed to just be the four of us.

As I stared down the tunnel of friends, confused, I saw Andrew, on the opposite end, all of a sudden get down on one knee.

Wait, was I getting proposed to in the "default world"? (The "default world" is what people who go to Burning Man call the "real world.")

As I walked through the tunnel of smiling friends, tears open-fauceting down my face, my eyes locked with Andrew's and in that moment, six years of our yearbooks played in my brain like a slideshow on one of those old Kodak projectors. (Andrew has made me a yearbook every single year since we met, and it's the book we turn to when we get into silly arguments and the occasional Atom Bomb fight. Andrew consistently keeps fresh in our minds how special our lives are through the snapshots in the book he painstakingly assembles each year. A picture truly is worth a thousand words, eh?)

I couldn't believe I had called in my very own **SNAG** to love and to love me back.

A **SNAG** is a **Secure New Age Guy** who has tapped into both his masculine and his feminine sides. He is strong yet sensitive, loves exploring, and enjoys mindfulness and culture. He is openly able to share feelings, shed tears, and not feel emasculated when his partner tells him what they like in bed. A SNAG is someone who really loves learning and growing as a human and never thinks he's done growing. He is not only willing to do the work on himself, but he is *excited* to unlock more within himself. He is secure enough to find authentic joy in his partner's accomplishments instead of being jealous of them or competing with them. A SNAG only compares himself with the previous version of himself. (Note: "SNAG" can stand for Secure New Age Gal too!)

I thought about the struggles Andrew and I had in the beginning with intimacy, and how that changed our relationship completely for the better because he was able to learn how to be present in the bedroom. I cherished him for putting in the effort to listen to my needs, I cherished his *willingness to grow*, and I cherished myself for doing the same.

My SNAG also was unafraid to commit to growing together, and we even had Lauren, my coach, set up a "Love Contract" for us.

THE LOVE CONTRACT

Our Love Contract became the guidepost for our relationship. A "Love Contract" is basically an agreement that two people get into and hold sacred. This way both parties never take each other for granted and both sign off on each rule as a commitment to one another. We had Lauren mediate ours, and it really makes sense to have a third party involved. Think of this as similar to marriage vows, but expressed only to one another and the mediator. (Although feel free to share your Love Contract with your friends so they can help hold your agreement sacred too.) Some of the agreements include things like sex two to three times per week (I would like to have sex more than Andrew, so we met in the middle and agreed to this amount), two date nights a week, four compliments a day, and no phones in the bedroom (your body needs a break from the Wi-Fi and radiation during the night anyway).

And here's the kicker: If you don't follow the agreement, there are real consequences! For example, if you bring your phone into the bedroom, you need to buy dinner for the other person that night. The consequences are not "angry" consequences, they are fun consequences.

Side note: For some reason, some people say it's "unsexy to schedule sex" and "it removes spontaneity," but that's just not true. If two people are busy, "sexy love hangs" must be scheduled.

"I would love to put a 'Love Contract' together but all the men I seem to attract are assholes. How do I even snag me a SNAG?"

To that I say: You often don't get a complete SNAG right off the bat, but there will be parts of them that are available right away. The most important thing is the *willingness* to grow. It's on you thereafter to show them the way! Ask for what you want, doing it gently and reminding them often.

The good news is that since women are gaining more and more strength within ourselves, and since we are primary or co-bread-winners now, we have the ability to choose the right partner who does exhibit more of the qualities of a SNAG.

"What do you think the first step should be to turn a PM into a SNAG?" I asked Elana Meta, the creator of Wild Vessel (an immersive experience to empower the feminine).

"I think it's all about creating the right space for men to feel safe enough to be vulnerable."

"What does that look like?"

"It's bringing in an open, loving energy and asking questions that tap into their vulnerable space."

"Like what?"

"What I mean by bringing in open, loving energy is focusing on who I am being in the conversation first, that is, embodying feelings of 'I am love,' 'I am safe,' and speaking from there. So when you want to help someone open up, close your eyes and feel yourself becoming a safe space and breathe into it. And then when it comes to the questions, it's just simple things—like 'How are you feeling?' and 'I'd love to hear how you feel about X'—to more intimate questions, when the time feels right, about their upbringing, like 'Tell me about your relationship with your mom' and 'How is your relationship with your dad?' And then just listen openly and give them space to feel things again. The more they trust that the space you have created is one where they can openly share their feelings, the more they will emote. If you just start there, you'll uncover a lot."

"Will this help men remove their 'masks of masculinity' once and for all?"

"It will certainly start to heal some of the trauma that has been suppressed, avoided, and disregarded for years. These traumatic feelings have been kept in the dark for a long time, unable to come out. When people talk about 'bringing light' to something, it's basically bringing attention to it, and energy naturally follows attention. So when you bring attention to a thing, you bring energy to it and then you can start moving and healing traumas that have been suppressed in the body for a long time."

On the other hand, when women are dealing with really tough PMs whose masks of masculinity are seemingly glued onto their faces and they seem impossible to crack open, we can resort to practicing what I've coined the "Bonobo Ape Method."

THE BONOBO APE METHOD

Female bonobo apes have a very strong bond with other female bonobos. Whenever there is an aggressive male bonobo that tries to get with a female bonobo, the females all come together and shun the male, making him go away. Thus an aggressive male bonobo will rarely (if ever) procreate with a female bonobo and will most likely die a lonely, miserable death by himself. Female bonobos choose to procreate with only the kindest, gentlest, most loving male bonobos, and in one generation, the females can transform an otherwise aggressive society into a kind, gentle, loving one.

Sooo ladies, can we learn from the female bonobos? Can we choose to procreate with the kindest, gentlest, most loving men and say no to those who haven't started to do the work on themselves and are unwilling to put in the time to learn what their partners want? Can we say no to the aggressive PMs who are holding on to their masks of masculinity tightly and aren't keen to tap into their vulnerable sides?

This way men will be forced to face themselves and learn to be vulnerable and ask questions in order to actually be able to have a partner and children at all.

SHOULD WE STICK WITH JUST ONE SNAG?

I went back and forth deciding if I wanted to include the next section in this book and concluded that the whole point of this book is to get us all out of our comfort zones fully and disrupt our status-quo thinking in all aspects of our lives, so I do hope you read these ideas with an open mind and heart. Please be reminded to remove all self-judgment and judgment of others as you read.

Okay, so now that we've figured out how to help reveal the SNAG-aliciousness in our men and are choosing only kind, gentle, SECURE men as our baseline, I'd love to explore the current monogamous belief structure that we live in.

A lot of men (and women too, but mostly men) in long-term relationships "fantasize" about having a second lover, and often the argument that men have is "men are built to spread our seed, whereas women are built to have one mate."

Looking back, the ethnographic evidence suggests that the way humans mated was predominantly "polygynous" (one husband, multiple wives) yet fairly recently, concrete evidence is showing "polyandrous" unions too (one wife, multiple husbands). Polyandry would make sense for maintaining family-owned land, spreading seed in societies where fertile women were scarce, etc.

Interestingly, almost all the writings about polyandry show it working only if the first or "main" husband controls the union between the wife and the second husband. It makes sense that this perspective is all we can find because pretty much all anthropologists at the time the research was done were men, and they couldn't fathom the idea of the woman controlling a polyandrous relationship.

Cut to today.

I have friends where the female has multiple male partners. For one friend, one man is her main husband and she has a second long-term partner. She has been with both of them for 25 years, and both men are friends. *She* made the decision to be with both of them, and both men agreed because they love her. Another female friend of mine has a long-term husband of 20 years and multiple lovers. Another female friend is in a long-term relationship with a man and she has a girlfriend that she and her husband invite into their relationship on her terms.

As long as everyone and everything is consensual, why is it not societally acceptable to try different and new things with different partners? Andrew and I are happily monogamous (and have been for the past six years) and might be this way forever, but we can't fully predict the future. And why should anyone else care what we do in various times of our relationship if everyone involved consents? If I want to have two husbands, a boyfriend, a girlfriend, and a sex partner, who is to say I can't have all that if everyone involved is down? It makes no sense to me that people judge others in any way if it's all consensual. Why should this short life be limited to only one school of thought, unless we want it and love it that way? Who made the rules? Who wrote the rule book? When was the rule book written? And why are we following those rules, again? Why can't everyone do what they want to do if everyone is consenting? It *just* doesn't make sense, does it?!

That monogamous relationships are seen as the only acceptable way of existing in the world because of old conditioning, patterns, and beliefs is exactly why we should feel free to disrupt all of it.

The one thing to note is that "humans appear prone, on average, to sexual jealousy, and so it would not be unreasonable for many of us—men and women alike—to project an assumption that sexual jealousy would make poly-unions untenable. Indeed, anthropologists have found that in both polyandry (one woman, multiple husbands) and polygyny (one husband, multiple wives), sexual jealousy often functions as a stressor in families around the world."[1]

"Okay, so let's just say two people have been in a monogamous relationship for years and one of them reads a book about having multiple partners and is curious about it. What do you do now?" I asked Elana.

"It's on the person who is curious to make the other person feel incredibly safe in just having the conversation. So if the person who is curious about it comes into the conversation aggressively, saying, 'This book said this and we should try it because I want to and why are you being so closed-minded?!,' that's not creating a safe space, is it? It becomes all about what the book said and about 'doing' versus how you are 'being'—how you are coming into the conversation and approaching this sensitive subject. It's on you to create the safe container."

"What if the person who is on the receiving end isn't into it?"

"It's important for both sides to openly communicate what feelings come up for them and why they feel the way they do. If the person receiving is not ready to talk about it, perhaps the person who is more curious will create a safe space for the receiver to learn more about it in a fun, inviting way. The key thing is safety and respect. The minute the curious one goes behind the receiver's back, trust gets lost and things will start to fall apart. Both parties have to love each other entirely and completely respect each other's desires and where they are."

A Disrupt-Her is always open to learning more and getting curious about worlds that she may not understand. She is not judging any of it and doesn't have to act on anything right away, but she is open to always exploring, because that sounds way more fun than being closed off and saying NO immediately, right?

TANTRA WITH YOUR SNAG

Now that we have created a safe space for our SNAGs to start fully self-expressing, and we have opened ourselves up to having conversations about all possibilities in the relationship, exploring and disrupting sex is the next frontier!

The first thing to master together is breathing.

I remember the first time I went to a yoga class at Yoga to the People. When I got there, the people to the left and right of me were making all kinds of loud sighing sounds and blubbering their lips and generally being loud with their breath. It felt really annoying to me at first, because I wanted to be on my yoga mat and relax into it, and that was really hard with everyone around me making all kinds of different (and, at the time, weird) noises.

I think so much of why that was frustrating in the past is that we often don't make different sounds in the world. There are socially acceptable sounds to make and there are not. Making orgasm sounds in public à la the *When Harry Met Sally* moment is simply mortifying to think about, right?

After a few yoga classes, I became accustomed to the loud, intentional sighing and breathing sounds and grew to love them. Breathing loudly really helped me bring more oxygen into my body, and I knew if it was beneficial during yoga practice, it would be beneficial in pretty much all situations. I often forget to breathe deeply because I've been so accustomed to going, going, going in the business world, so I now set reminders on my phone every couple of hours to take three long, deep breaths. Just doing this helps stabilize my nervous system and grounds me.

Andrew and I also realized that learning how to breathe during sex was the key ingredient in having the most fully embodied orgasms. Barbara Carrellas from Urban Tantra had the perfect audio class for us to listen to and practice with, and I recommend it to everyone. What clicked for both of us was when Barbara talked about the concept of "quick and quiet." We have been led to think that sex is "naughty" and "bad" and since boys especially start watching porn at such a young age, not only are they negatively conditioned by watching porn itself (because it's realllly not how most women want to have sex), they have also been conditioned to be quick and quiet to get it over with. You'll notice yourself holding your breath often during sex instead of breathing into the orgasm or into the sexual experience. Observe yourself and see how often you forget to breathe!

In my tantra class, I started breathing loudly, starting from my root chakra and moving all the way up to my throat chakra, and I have never had more deep or full-body orgasms in my life. And all of this from just breathing!

It's amazing what happens when we first wipe away the self-judgment and judgment of others and then give ourselves permission to disrupt the way we have been conditioned to do things like choosing mates, breathing, and having sex. We *can choose* only kind, loving SNAGs to breed with, we *can choose* to explore our sexuality with a fresh perspective, and we *can choose* to breathe differently if we want to. That's what makes all of this so. Much. Fun. Even Maria Soledad, a powerful energy expert, said: if we can just stop holding on to patterns, beliefs, and conditioning from centuries past, we will be liberated to be fully who we want to be.

PUTTING IT ALL TOGETHER

To be a Disrupt-Her, you must (1) get back to your childlike state of curiosity, playfulness, and awe; (2) practice addition by subtraction in all facets of your life; (3) figure out what your LIT path is as opposed to a traditional "career path"; (4) start investing your money wisely; (5) become a Warrior Gatekeeper of your mind by actively catching what comes to your mental gate (and then practicing pattern interruption if you do accidentally let in a negative thought and start spiraling out of control); (6) iterate and get better every day in all the things you're doing, instead of focusing on being perfect; (7) catch yourself when you're being a Hate-Her by understanding where you are in your life personally and where you are not in integrity; (8) embody your Disrupt-Her spirit wholeheartedly by improving the world in your own way; (9) define feminism for yourself, and help men remove their masks of masculinity using the Triple-Q technique and by loving and supporting them when they show their emotional side; (10) give yourself full permission to expose ALL your Shakti goddesses in business and in life; (11) replace the word "failure" with "revelation" and never skip the postmortem part of the process; and (12) exclusively choose a SNAG as a mate, remove partners who don't lift you up, and keep an open mind when thinking about sex and relationship structures.

DISRUPTION #12

EXERCISES

1. Take some time to identify the SNAG characteristics in your partner. Write them down on paper. If things are missing and you are not feeling fully supported, have an open, honest (nonaccusatory!) conversation with him. And if he is still not responding well, perhaps it's time for you to move on! The most important thing is for partners to be *willing* to grow! Follow the example of the bonobo apes!

2. Create a Love Contract with your partner. Have fun with it!

3. Practice breathing intentionally during the day, and breathing out loud. Breathe in for a count of four. Hold your breath for two counts, and then breathe out for six counts. Bring that to the bedroom.

4. Do fun new things like a weekly tantra listening session (download Barbara Carrellas's audio recordings from Urban Tantra) with your partner, and do it along with a group of friends who are in relationships so you can hold each other accountable.

5. Promise to have an open mind. Life's too short.

RB ACCOUNTABILIBUDDY
ACTION #12!

READY TO SNAG YOUR SNAG?

THIS IS THE MOMENT WHEN YOU FEEL
YOUR FEMALE POWER OVERCOME YOUR BODY
AND RECOGNIZE THAT YOU HOLD THE POWER OF
HUMANITY INSIDE YOUR WOMB.
WITH THIS REALIZATION, YOU CAN INVITE IN ONLY
THE KINDEST, GENTLEST, MOST SECURE PARTNER
TO BE WITH. AND ONCE YOU MEET THE RIGHT KIND SOUL,
IMAGINE IF YOU HAD THE ABILITY TO GROW TOGETHER IN
AN UNLIMITED WAY BECAUSE BOTH OF YOU ARE EXCITED
TO GROW? FIND THE PERSON WHO IS WILLING TO DO
THE WORK AND YOU CAN HELP OPEN HIM UP TO
BECOMING THE PRINCE OF YOUR DREAMS.

SO WHENEVER YOU FIND YOURSELF ON A DATE WITH
A PM AND WANT TO SEE IF HE IS WILLING TO SHOW SIGNS
OF A SNAG, RB IS ASKING YOU TO PUT YOUR INDEX FINGER
UNDERNEATH HER AND RUN YOUR FINGER AROUND HER.
WHILE DOING THAT, ASK HIM THREE QUESTIONS THAT
ANDREW HORN, MY PARTNER AND SOCIAL FLOW EXPERT, ASKS:

WHAT ARE YOU EXCITED ABOUT?
WHAT ARE YOU STRUGGLING WITH?
HOW ARE YOU MOST LIKE YOUR MOM/DAD?

YOU'LL LEARN A LOT ABOUT WHO HE IS BY HIS ANSWERS.
IS HE EXCITED ABOUT WHAT HE'S WORKING ON
ONLY BECAUSE OF SELF-GAIN, MONEY, OR POWER,
OR BECAUSE HE WANTS TO HELP IMPROVE HIMSELF,
HIS COMMUNITY, OR THE WORLD IN SOME WAY?
IS HE SELF-AWARE ENOUGH TO SHARE WHAT
HE IS STRUGGLING WITH?
IS IT SHALLOW?   IS IT DEEP?   IS HE SELF-AWARE ENOUGH
TO UNDERSTAND HOW HE'S MOST LIKE HIS MOM AND DAD?
ARE HIS ANSWERS GENUINE OR PUT ON?

ALSO, IF HE DOESN'T ASK YOU ANY QUESTIONS BACK,
THAT'S NOT A GREAT SIGN . . .

DRAW A LINE IN THE MATING SAND ABOUT THE
KIND OF PERSON YOU CHOOSE. IF ALL WOMEN CHOOSE
SNAGS, IN ONE GENERATION WE CAN CHANGE THE WORLD!

DISRUPTION #13

COMMON BELIEF

Have your best poker face on in life
and keep the challenges quiet.

DISRUPTION

It's all about transparency,
vulnerability, and
community.

"Think we should postpone?" Andrew wondered. "It's literally a torrential storm outside. Also, everyone is hungover from Halloween . . ."

"No, let's keep it. Even if only a handful of people show up, it will be worth it."

Andrew had sent out an e-mail three days prior inviting our good friends to a celebratory "victory dinner" at my restaurant in Williamsburg, The Greenhouse at WILD. We were celebrating the sale of some of my shares in THINX, because we believe it is important to imprint victorious moments in our lives and create positive rituals around them. My favorite ritual is to gather my friends and share a great meal. I was SO excited to treat my friends to dinner, since they had been with me along the crazy roller-coaster ride.

After we got to Wild, people started to come in one by one and two by two, and all of a sudden, there were 30 of my closest friends in the back greenhouse chatting and catching up with one another.

I looked around and took a deep breath to capture this moment. I had spent years nurturing most of these friendships through thick and thin, ups and downs, and this tribe was truly my family. They showed up on a rainy, cold, windy Sunday because they couldn't pass up a celebration of one of their besties. I was so proud of this community. Everyone in the room was doing something to impact the world positively and was on a quest of self-development; they did not take their lives for granted; and most importantly, they showed up for one another when asked.

I took another deep breath to imprint my surroundings on my memory. I spent years working in my restaurants to do my best to create a great experience for people so they too could deepen their relationships while eating healthy food. It was the *hardest business in the world*, and it taught me SO much about business and how to deal with people (like hangry customers!), and I thought to myself, *What better place to hold a victory dinner than where it all began?*

Andrew, as he always does, stood up and called for everyone's attention to unify the conversation. Whenever our community gathered over dinner, we always did this so everyone could be in one conversation (instead of many side conversations). It strengthened the connection and created a sacred space between everyone in the room, and it became a ritualized practice that our crew looked forward to.

Andrew then shared some words about his experience being by my side through the rise and fall of my time at THINX, and he invited everyone to share their favorite memory from the entrepreneurial journey, be it a high or a low.

Allie went first: "You pioneered a conversation when nobody wanted to. You fought so hard, and against all odds, including total pushback from society to get this message out. And there are now millions of women around the world who are more confident around their bodies and their periods because of your relentlessness."

Radha went second: "Talk is cheap. Execution is everything. Lots of people have ideas, but rarely do people actually follow through. And you did."

Max followed: "I remember when the NYC public transit system tried to ban your advertisements in the subway for using the word 'period,' and instead of getting upset, you got super excited about it and knew that this was the opportunity to get the company some real press. And the story went viral, and it put the company on the map."

I started crying. The past six years of hard work to get the product created with my co-founders, then the uphill battle to get the product out into the world (and the battle to get people to change their habits); then the battle to get the press to even talk about it, then the battle to change culture around the most taboo subject in the world; then the battle at the very end as I transitioned out as C.E.O., culminating in the sale of my shares . . . all piled on me like soccer players after a victorious goal in a long-fought match. What a journey, what lessons, what blessings, and what strength it all gave me. I cried with the utmost gratitude.

The comments that came next were actually the most surprising part to me:

"I happened to be at your house when you got the call from the lawyers. I watched you fight like a warrior, and in between, you instructed me to massage your feet while you were on the call." Everyone laughed.

"I also remember coming over right when you were about to hit SEND on a super-important e-mail, and you asked me to review it. I couldn't believe you trusted me enough to go over such a tough e-mail just like that."

"I too happened to be at your house when you had to deal with another tough legal call. It gave me fire in my belly as I watched you fight for the truth and for what you believed in. You never wavered. You cried in my arms after, but never wavered during."

"I loved seeing you as I was walking into the gym and you were walking out and you had just got off the phone from what was clearly a rough call. When you saw me, your eyes welled up and I remember taking you to Juice Generation to get an acai bowl and talk it through. I felt so honored that you shared what you were going through so openly, and it gave me strength to deal with tougher times too."

And it went on like that, one after another. None of it was about the "meteoric rise of the company," or how much money I made for the company, or making the cover of *Entrepreneur* magazine. It was all about how my friends witnessed me during the toughest times, the intense struggles, the crazy battles, all the way through to the media-created "fall from grace." My friends expressed their gratitude for being able to be literally next to me when I cried, grieved, fought, and sat silently dumbfounded at what was being said, and not one of my friends took my transparency and vulnerability for granted. Instead they were as grateful for it as I was grateful to have been given the space to feel through it all with them holding crucial space for me.

As this book comes to a close and your disruptive journey takes off to magical places you never thought possible, one of the final defining things to note is that disruption won't be possible without a tribe to support you. Revolutions and movements almost always happen when a group of people galvanizes *together*. If you don't have a tribe, join one that inspires you, one that is doing good things and is generative in the world. Show up, participate often, bring new ideas to the conversations, organize fun things to do, listen intently, be there for them when they are going through shit, and clap so hard for them when they have a win—and you'll have a tribe in no time. You'll come to realize that no money, fame, or power could trump having a loving community that supports the shit out of you, even though the current patriarchal society is telling you otherwise. We often forget what's important, and the goal of this book is *to remember* and then take real, tangible action to get there.

The most important realization I had post–victory dinner was that to truly be a Disrupt-Her means that we have to lay it *all* on the table. And I mean ALLLLL. The more transparent and vulnerable we are through it *all*, the more our tribe can support us, and the faster we can come back stronger and wiser for the next go-round. Because there is *always* a next go-round for the Disrupt-Her.

The Disrupt-Her deeply knows how to shift the idea of "struggle" from something negative and hard to something exciting and generative, seeing an opportunity to break new ground. Because in the end, it's the moments of struggle that define us.

IT'S THE MOMENTS OF
STRUGGLE THAT INSPIRE
TRUE TRANSFORMATION.

IT'S THE MOMENTS
OF STRUGGLE THAT
LEAD TO THE BIGGEST
BREAKTHROUGHS.

IT'S THE MOMENTS OF
STRUGGLE THAT INSPIRE
THOSE AROUND US.

IT'S THE MOMENTS OF
STRUGGLE AND RELENTLESS
DETERMINATION THAT
IMPACT THE WORLD.

Now it's your turn.

It's your turn to truly question, challenge, and then disrupt all aspects of your life, struggles and all, so you can live a more excited, impassioned, lit-up existence filled with adventure, love, friendship, and fulfilling work that creates a positive ripple effect for generations to come . . .

. . . And please hurry—this world needs you now!

RB ACCOUNTABILIBUDDY
ACTION #13!

YOU DID IT!! ALL RB IS ASKING YOU TO DO
IS TO GIVE YOURSELF A MASSIVE HUG FOR
GETTING TO THE END OF THIS BOOK
AND FOR CHOOSING TO DISRUPT YOUR LIFE.
BY FACING YOURSELF OVER AND OVER AGAIN
AND CHALLENGING YOUR OWN BELIEF SYSTEMS, PATTERN
AND SOCIETAL CONDITIONING, YOU WILL EXPERIENCE
THE MOST LIT-UP LIFE
IMAGINABLE AND INSPIRE THOSE AROUND
YOU TO DO THE SAME.

YOU WILL BE PROUD OF YOURSELF FOR
JUST BEING YOU BECAUSE YOU FINALLY REMOVED
ALL THE LAYERS TO GET BACK HOME TO YOURSELF.
CONGRATULATIONS FOR
GETTING BACK TO

JUST BEING YOU.

ENDNOTES

INTRODUCTION

1. Jim Clifton, "The World's Broken Workplace," *The Chairman's Blog*, Gallup, June 13, 2017, http://news.gallup.com/opinion/chairman/212045/world-broken-workplace.aspx.

2. Sarah Jane Glynn, "Breadwinning Mothers Are Increasingly the U.S. Norm," Center for American Progress, December 19, 2016, www.americanprogress.org/issues/women/reports/2016/12/19/295203/breadwinning-mothers-are-increasingly-the-u-s-norm.

3. Henry David Thoreau, *Walden: Or, Life in the Woods* (New York: Houghton Mifflin, 1906), 101.

4. Jon Krakauer, *Into the Wild* (New York: Anchor Books, 2007), 56–57.

5. https://papers.ssrn.com/sol3/papers.cfm?abstract_id=587201.

DISRUPTION #1

1. Judy Dutton, "In the Lab with the World's Leading Laugh Scientist," *Mental Floss*, March–April 2012, http://mentalfloss.com/article/30329/lab-worlds-leading-laugh-scientist.

2. Gordon MacKenzie, *Orbiting the Giant Hairball: A Corporate Fool's Guide to Surviving with Grace* (New York: Viking, 1998), 205.

DISRUPTION #2

1. Bronislaw Malinowski, *Argonauts of the Western Pacific* (New York: E. P. Dutton, 1922), 97. Quoted in Lewis Hyde, *The Gift: Creativity and the Artist in the Modern World* (New York: Random House, 2007), 18.

DISRUPTION #4

1. Valentina Zarya, "Venture Capital's Funding Gender Gap Is Actually Getting Worse," *Fortune*, March 13, 2017, http://fortune.com/2017/03/13/female-founders-venture-capital.

2. "Prove It Again!," Gender Bias Learning Project, www.genderbiasbingo.com/prove-it-again.

DISRUPTION #5

1. https://www.researchgate.net/publication/240826812_Why_People_Gossip_An_Empirical_Analysis_of_Social_Motives_Antecedents_and_Consequences.

2. http://www.news.gatech.edu/2012/06/06/have-you-heard-nearly-15-percent-work-email-gossip.

3. https://www.independent.co.uk/news/people/yusra-mardini-rio-2016-olympics-womens-swimming-the-syrian-refugee-competing-in-the-olympics-who-a7173546.html.

DISRUPTION #6

1. https://hbr.org/2014/08/why-women-dont-apply-for-jobs-unless-theyre-100-qualified.

2. Celena Chong, "Startups Founded by Women Are Doing Way Better Than Ones Founded by Men, Says Top Firm First Round Capital," *Business Insider*, July 30, 2015, www.businessinsider.com/female-founders-outperform-male-peers-2015-7.

3. Mark J. Perry, "Fortune 500 Firms 1955 v. 2016: Only 12% Remain, Thanks to the Creative Destruction That Fuels Economic Prosperity," AEI Ideas (blog), December 13, 2016, www.aei.org/publication/fortune-500-firms-1955-v-2016-only-12-remain-thanks-to-the-creative-destruction-that-fuels-economic-prosperity.

5. "Double Bind," Gender Bias Learning Project, www.genderbiasbingo.com/double-bind.

DISRUPTION #7

1. Zhana Vrangalova, Rachel E. Bukberg, and Gerulf Rieger, "Birds of a Feather? Not When It Comes to Sexual Permissiveness," *Journal of Social and Personal Relationships* 31, no. 1 (February 2014): 93–113, doi: 10.1177/0265407513487638.

2. N. R. Crick and M. A. Bigbee, "Relational and Overt Forms of Peer Victimization: A Multiinformant Approach," *Journal of Consulting and Clinical Psychology* 66, no. 2 (April 1998): 337–47.

3. Seth Meyers, "Women Who Hate Other Women: The Psychological Root of Snarky," *Psychology Today* blog, September 24, 2013, www.psychologytoday.com/us/blog/insight-is-2020/201309/women-who-hate-other-women-the-psychological-root-snarky.

4. Ibid.

5. "The History of Patriarchy," Women's Resource Center, University of Colorado–Boulder, February 13, 2015, www.colorado.edu/wrc/2015/02/13/history-patriarchy.

DISRUPTION #8

1. "English is read from left to right, but are some languages written from right to left or from top to bottom?" Dictionary.com, www.dictionary.com/e/righttoleft; "Why are more people right-handed?" *Scientific American*, August 18, 1997, www.scientificamerican.com/article/why-are-more-people-right.

DISRUPTION #9

1. Steve Taylor, "Why Men Oppress Women," *Psychology Today*, August 30, 2012, https://www.psychologytoday.com/us/blog/out-the-darkness/201208/why-men-oppress-women.

2. Catherine Oluyemo, "Challenges of Women Leadership in a Patriarchy Society: Implications for Development of African Women," paper delivered at the International Conference on Social Sciences, Amsterdam, August 7–8, 2014; abstract available at https://waset.org/abstracts/6547.

3. www.collinsdictionary.com/dictionary/english/feminism.

4. Gloria Steinem, "The Real Definition of Feminism, from Gloria Steinem," interview with Marlo Thomas, *Huffington Post*, February 25, 2013, www.huffingtonpost.com/2013/02/22/the-real-definition-of-feminism-marlo-thomas-mondays-with-marlo_n_2743593.html.

5. "Maternal Wall," Gender Bias Learning Project, www.genderbiasbingo.com/maternal-wall.

6. Jenny Anderson, "Huge Study Finds That Companies with More Women Leaders Are More Profitable," *Quartz*, February 8, 2016, https://qz.com/612086/huge-study-find-that-companies-with-more-women-leaders-are-more-profitable/.

7. https://en.wikipedia.org/wiki/Fourth-wave_feminism.

8. Janet Bloomfield, "Seven Things Feminists Hate to Hear and Absolutely Can't Talk About," *Thought Catalog*, April 21, 2015, https://thoughtcatalog.com/janet-bloomfield/2015/04/7-things-feminists-hate-to-hear.

9. Ronald F. Levant, "The Male Role Norms Inventory (MNRI) and Related Instruments," http://www.drronaldlevant.com/mrni.html.

10. bell hooks, *The Will to Change* (New York: Atria Books, 2004), 11.

DISRUPTION #10

1. Barefoot Bob, "The Native American Sweatlodge: A Spiritual Tradition," www.wakingtimes.com/2013/05/25/the-native-american-sweatlodge-a-spiritual-tradition/.

2. Jean Johnson, "Shakti: The Power of the Feminine," Asia Society, http://asiasociety.org/education/shakti-power-feminine.

3. Ibid.

4. "The Four Principles of Conscious Capitalism," Conscious Capitalism, www.consciouscapitalism.org.

5. Gay Hendricks, *The Big Leap* (New York: HarperCollins, 2009).

DISRUPTION #11

1. http://www.dictionary.com/browse/scout?s=t.

2. Claire Groden, "Why Women Are Afraid of Failure," *Elle*, June 6, 2016, www.elle.com/life-love/a36828/why-women-are-afraid-of-failure.

3. Victoria L Brescoll, Erica Dawson, Eric Luis Uhlmann, "Hard Won and Easily Lost: The Fragile Status of Leaders in Gender-Stereotype-Incongruent Occupations," Gender Action Portal, Harvard Kennedy School, http://gap.hks.harvard.edu/hard-won-and-easily-lost-fragile-status-leaders-gender-stereotype-incongruent-occupations.

4. http://www.dictionary.com/browse/failing.

5. http://www.dictionary.com/browse/revelation?s=t.

DISRUPTION #12

1. Alice Dreger, "When Taking Multiple Husbands Makes Sense," *Atlantic*, February 1, 2013, www.theatlantic.com/health/archive/2013/02/when-taking-multiple-husbands-makes-sense/272726.

ACKNOWLEDGMENTS

First I'd like to acknowledge Andrew Horn, my husband, my baby daddy, and the big-hearted SNAG, for consistently holding space for me through the wild ride of the creative, entrepreneurial process. Seven years and counting, thank you for tenderly clasping my hand through this great adventure of life. This book would never have been made possible without your love and endless support. And thank you to your sperm for meeting my egg which created the most magical creature of all time.

To Radha—my twin sister—thank you for being my first "Disrupt-Her partner in crime," starting in mama's womb, and also for being my co-conspirator and champion in all that I do. I love that you keep me on my toes, even when we fight, and make me want to kick ass every day.

To Mama and Daddy—my parents—thank you for raising me to believe that I could create any reality for myself if I just put energy toward it. Thank you for being the first role models for what's possible and for choosing to dedicate a massive chunk of your lives to support and nurture mine. Thank you for also teaching me to never, ever give up.

To Yuri and Ben—my sister and brother-in-law—thank you for putting up with me and for inspiring me by your unwavering dedication to your important work in medicine and the environment and for your quiet leadership. And of course, thank you for creating the badass that is Emi. Excited for Alice Emerson!

To Sam Horn—my mother-in-law—thank you for being my sensei in my writing journey. Thank you for giving me confidence that I could be a writer and for patiently helping me work through each chapter. I will also forever be grateful that you spent the first four months of Hiro's life sacrificing your sleep and your own work to ease us into the HOLY SHITNESS of becoming parents. I will never forget that.

To Lauren Zander—my life and leadership coach—thank you for holding me accountable in every aspect of my life and for teaching me how to deal with the challenging parts with a laugh! You're the only one who can kick my ass in the way that you do and make me beg for more!

To my amazing friends—Boom Spiral and beyond—you know who you are—thank you for bringing so much adventure, fun, inspiration, great conversations, and laughter to my life. And for being SO there for me through the roller coaster of life.

To my Wild restaurant business partner, Walid—thank you for showing me what incredible partnership looks like and for being the best restaurateur I know with the highest integrity. (They're hard to find!)

To my teams for my companies—thank you for bringing so much creativity, passion, and energy to our disruptive products. We are challenging the status quo and changing culture every day! I'm so proud to be working with you.

To my investors, suppliers, and vendors—thank you for believing in my zany ideas at every stage and for giving energy to all of it.

To my Conscious Capitalism Board—for showing me how to truly think about business in a conscious way and for continuing to fight the good fight.

To my editors at Hay House—Anne and Patty—and to my agents at SLL—Celeste, Sarah, and Anna—thank you for believing in me and this book, even when shit was crazy, and for dedicating your time and energy into making this book the most impactful it could be.

To the amazing artist Taylor for creating the beautiful, artful images and Jake for making them possible and to Daniel for taking the beautiful photographs.

To Mother Earth, for gifting us your life force that nourishes us all. I will forever fight for you.

Finally, thank YOU to you for reading this book and for courageously shining a light on your own shit so you can be the most disruptive, alive human possible. GO YOU FOR DOING IT!

ABOUT THE AUTHOR

Miki Agrawal is a serial social entrepreneur. She was the recipient of the Tribeca Film Festival's Disruptive Innovation Award, she was named 2017 Young Global Leader by World Economic Forum and Social Entrepreneur of the Year by the World Technology Summit, she was one of *INC* magazine's Most Impressive Women Entrepreneurs of 2016, *Forbes*'s Top 20 Millennials on a Mission, and made the cover of *Entrepreneur* magazine in 2016.

She is the founder of the acclaimed farm-to-table, alternative pizza concept called WILD (www.eatdrinkwild.com) with three locations in New York City, one in Guatemala, and more on the way.

She co-founded and built THINX, a high-tech, period-proof underwear brand, and led the company as C.E.O. to *Fast Company*'s Most Innovative Companies of 2017, helping tens of millions of women period better. She also co-founded Icon, a high-tech pee-proof underwear brand that helps women manage light bladder leakage.

She most recently founded TUSHY (www.hellotushy.com), a company that is revolutionizing the American toilet category with a modern, affordable designer bidet attachment that both upgrades human health and hygiene and protects the environment from wasteful toilet paper consumption. She and her team are also helping fight the global sanitation crisis by bringing clean latrines to underserved communities in India through their partnership with Samagra.

She is the author of *Do Cool Sh*t*, a book on entrepreneurship and lifestyle design.

Miki is an identical twin, half-Japanese, half-Indian French Canadian, former professional soccer player, graduate of Cornell University, and proud new mama of Hiro Happy.

Website: www.mikiagrawal.com

Hay House Titles of Related Interest

YOU CAN HEAL YOUR LIFE, the movie,
starring Louise Hay & Friends
(available as a 1-DVD program, an expanded 2-DVD set,
and an online streaming video)
Learn more at www.hayhouse.com/louise-movie

THE SHIFT, the movie,
starring Dr. Wayne W. Dyer
(available as a 1-DVD program, an expanded 2-DVD set,
and an online streaming video)
Learn more at www.hayhouse.com/the-shift-movie

———

DODGING ENERGY VAMPIRES:
An Empath's Guide to Evading Relationships That Drain You
and Restoring Your Health and Power,
by Christiane Northrup, M.D.

PUSSY: A Reclamation,
by Regena Thomashauer

RISE SISTER RISE:
A Guide to Unleashing the Wise, Wild Woman Within,
by Rebecca Campbell

WOMEN ROCKING BUSINESS:
The Ultimate Step-by-Step Guidebook to Create a Thriving Life Doing Work
You Love, by Sage Lavine

All of the above are available at your local bookstore,
or may be ordered by contacting Hay House (see next page).

———

We hope you enjoyed this Hay House book. If you'd like to receive our online catalog featuring additional information on Hay House books and products, or if you'd like to find out more about the Hay Foundation, please contact:

Hay House, Inc., P.O. Box 5100, Carlsbad, CA 92018-5100
(760) 431-7695 or (800) 654-5126
(760) 431-6948 (fax) or (800) 650-5115 (fax)
www.hayhouse.com® • www.hayfoundation.org

———

Published in Australia by:
Hay House Australia Pty. Ltd., 18/36 Ralph St., Alexandria NSW 2015
Phone: 612-9669-4299 • *Fax:* 612-9669-4144 • www.hayhouse.com.au

Published in the United Kingdom by:
Hay House UK, Ltd., Astley House, 33 Notting Hill Gate, London W11 3JQ
Phone: 44-20-3675-2450 • *Fax:* 44-20-3675-2451 • www.hayhouse.co.uk

Published in India by: Hay House Publishers India,
Muskaan Complex, Plot No. 3, B-2, Vasant Kunj, New Delhi 110 070
Phone: 91-11-4176-1620 • *Fax:* 91-11-4176-1630 • www.hayhouse.co.in

———

Access New Knowledge.
Anytime. Anywhere.

Learn and evolve at your own pace
with the world's leading experts.

www.hayhouseU.com

Free e-newsletters
from Hay House, the Ultimate
Resource for Inspiration

Be the first to know about Hay House's free downloads, special offers, giveaways, contests, and more!

 Get exclusive excerpts from our latest releases and videos from *Hay House Present Moments*.

 Our *Digital Products Newsletter* is the perfect way to stay up-to-date on our latest discounted eBooks, featured mobile apps, and Live Online and On Demand events.

 Learn with real benefits! *HayHouseU.com* is your source for the most innovative online courses from the world's leading personal growth experts. Be the first to know about new online courses and to receive exclusive discounts.

 Enjoy uplifting personal stories, how-to articles, and healing advice, along with videos and empowering quotes, within *Heal Your Life*.

 Have an inspirational story to tell and a passion for writing? Sharpen your writing skills with insider tips from *Your Writing Life*.

Sign Up Now!

Get inspired, educate yourself, get a complimentary gift, and share the wisdom!

Visit www.hayhouse.com/newsletters to sign up today!

HAY HOUSE

HAYHOUSE
RADIO
radio for your soul®

HAYHOUSE
online learning